Brenda Chamberlain was born in Bangor in 1912. In 1931 she went to train as a painter at the Royal Academy Schools in London and five years later, after marrying the artist-craftsman John Petts, settled near the village of Llanllechid, near Bethesda in Caernarfonshire. During the Second World War, while working as a guide searching Snowdonia for lost aircraft, she temporarily gave up painting in favour of poetry and worked, with her husband, on the production of the Caseg Broadsheets, a series of six which included poems by Dylan Thomas, Alun Lewis and Lynette Roberts. In 1947, her marriage ended, she went to live on Bardsey (Ynys Enlli), a small island off the tip of the Llŷn Peninsula, where she remained until 1961. After six years on the Greek island of Ídra (Hydra), she returned to Bangor. She died there in 1971. She described the rigours and excitements of her life on Bardsey in *Tide-race* (1962) and the island also inspired many of her paintings. Her book of poems, *The Green Heart* (1958), contains work that reflects her life in Llanllechid, on Bardsey and in Germany. Her German experiences are portrayed in her novel *The Water-Castle* (1964). *A Rope of Vines* was published in 1965; *Poems with Drawings* in 1969; and *Alun Lewis and the Making of the Caseg Broadsheets* in 1970.

T0150609

Frontispiece: Brenda Chamberlain by Emyr Roberts, September 1968.
© Emyr Roberts.

The Protagonists

Brenda Chamberlain

Edited by Damian Walford Davies

PARTHIAN

Parthian
The Old Surgery
Napier Street
Cardigan
SA43 1ED
www.parthianbooks.com

First published in 2013
The Protagonists © Brenda Chamberlain
'Introduction' and all other material
© Damian Walford Davies, 2013
All Rights Reserved

ISBN 978-1-908069-96-2

The publisher acknowledges the financial support
of the Welsh Books Council.

Edited by Damian Walford Davies

Cover design and typesetting by Claire Houguez
Cover image: based on Greek Poster Art, early 1970s
Back Cover Image: Brenda Chamberlain by Emyr Roberts,
September 1968. © Emyr Roberts.

Printed and bound by www.lightningsource.com

British Library Cataloguing in Publication Data

A cataloguing record for this book is available from the British Library.

In memory of David Lyn
(1927-2012)

Contents

Acknowledgements

A number of individuals have given me invaluable assistance and advice in preparing this first published edition of Brenda Chamberlain's play, *The Protagonists*. I am grateful to Manos Antoninis, Richard Davies, Lynn C. Francis, Lucy Gough, Rebecca Gould, Owen Garmon, John Hefin, David Lyn, Reuven Jasser, Sara Jones, Jill Piercy, Joy Ostle, Emyr Roberts, Francesca Rhydderch, David Trotter, and Jason Walford Davies.

For permission to quote Chamberlain's published and unpublished work, I am grateful to the executor of the estate, Reuven Jasser. The text of *The Protagonists* held at the Gwynedd Archives and Museums Service, Caernarfon Record Office, is used by kind permission of the Head Archivist, Lynn C. Francis. Brenda Chamberlain's manuscripts are quoted by permission of Llyfrgell Genedlaethol Cymru/The National Library of Wales.

An award from the Aberystwyth University Research Fund, for which I am very grateful, expedited the project.

I have benefited greatly from the work of those scholars and commentators who have assessed Brenda Chamberlain's achievement as writer, poet and artist. The work of Kate Holman and Jill Piercy in particular has offered numerous insights.

My greatest debt is to Alan 'Phredd' McPherson, who played the Guard in the 1968 performances of *The Protagonists*. This edition would not have been possible without him. He most generously shared with me his acting script, which is at the heart of any understanding of how *The Protagonists* was staged. His readiness to answer a constant stream (often a Chamberlainian tide-race) of questions, together with his sharp evocation of the Bangor scene in the late 1960s and his insights into Brenda Chamberlain's imaginative world and personal circumstances were fascinating – and frequently moving.

List of Figures

Frontispiece (p. ii): Brenda Chamberlain by Emyr Roberts, September 1968. © Emyr Roberts.

Figure 1 (p. xxxvii): National Library of Wales, MS 21493D, p. 82 (third draft of *The Protagonists*). Chamberlain's drawing of the actors' 'positions a[t] this point' (i.e. O's line 'For once, I agree with you, maker of edicts'– see p. 35). Llyfrgell Genedlaethol Cymru/The National Library of Wales.

Figure 2 (p. xxxviii): National Library of Wales, MS 21492D, p. 5 (second draft of *The Protagonists*). Chamberlain's drawing of the view from her window on Ídhra, between a sketch of the prisoners' cells at the beginning of the play and the statement 'In this room, *The Protagonists* was written, Autumn 1967'. Llyfrgell Genedlaethol Cymru/The National Library of Wales.

Figures 3a and 3b (p. xl): programme leaflet for *The Protagonists*. Courtesy of Alan McPherson.

Figure 4 (p. xliii): Sophia Michopoulou (L) and Jeff Thompson (Z); September 1968 rehearsals. © Emyr Roberts.

Figure 5 (p. xliii): Around the central figure of Jeff Thompson (Z), from left: Gray Evans (O); David Lyn (Producer, standing in for Gwyn Parry, who played A); Alan McPherson (Guard); Vasilis Politis (H, head lowered); Owen Garmon (J); Sophia Michopoulou (L). September 1968 rehearsals. © Emyr Roberts.

Figure 6 (p. xliv): Alan McPherson (Guard, left); Vasilis Politis (H). September 1968 rehearsals. © Emyr Roberts.

Figure 7 (p. xliv): From left: Alan McPherson (Guard); Gray Evans (O); David Lyn (Producer); Owen Garmon (J). September 1968 rehearsals. © Emyr Roberts.

Figure 8 (p. xlvi): Alan McPherson as the Guard; dress rehearsal, October 1968.

Figure 9 (p. xlvii): 3-D reconstruction of the stage set for *The Protagonists* in Prichard-Jones Hall, University College of North Wales, Bangor, by Damian Walford Davies (Google SketchUp software), based on sketches in Katherine Elizabeth Holman, 'The Literary Achievement of Brenda Chamberlain' (unpublished MA thesis, University College of Swansea, 1976) and descriptions by Alan McPherson.

Figure 10 (p. xlviii): Publicity poster for *The Protagonists*. By kind permission of Emyr Roberts.

Figure 11 (p. xlviii): Publicity poster for *The Protagonists*: detail of Chamberlain's drawing-collage. By kind permission of Emyr Roberts.

Figure 12 (p. lxxvi): National Library of Wales, ex 2735: cover of the annotated acting script belonging to Alan ('Phredd') McPherson. By kind permission of Alan McPherson.

Figure 13 (p. 4): National Library of Wales MS 21493D, p. 11: Brenda Chamberlain's drawing of the prisoners' attitudes at the beginning of *The Protagonists*, from the third version of the play. Llyfrgell Genedlaethol Cymru/The National Library of Wales.

Introduction

It is there from the start of Brenda Chamberlain's career as artist, poet, writer and dramatist: the compulsion to reflect on boundaries both hard and permeable, on the condition of 'islandness', and on the constant need she felt for 'communication across "deep water"'.[1] From the 1960s until her untimely death in 1971, these central preoccupations took the form of a generically diverse but intellectually cohesive cartography of Europe's militarised fronts and patrolled borders that gives the lie to the orthodox view of her as a writer of merely 'rudimentary' (and late-flowering) political convictions whose work eschews ideological debate.[2] Moreover, her imaginative maps are always acute emotional geographies: aware of the ways in which physical space conditions our inner, creative lives, Chamberlain was from the outset a smart psychogeographer.

It is time to recognise the geographical reach, cultural depth and profound connectedness of Chamberlain's European archipelago. In Tony Conran's evocative, punning phrase, she was 'Star Chamberlain of islands'.[3] Her actual and imagined island coordinates range from the lyrical 'ethnoscapes' of J. M. Synge's Aran and the Isle of Man (she was Manx and Irish by blood, Welsh only by birth), to the humpbacked Bardsey of her fabling autobiography, *Tide-race* (1962) and the moated German landscapes and border zones of her eerie, genre-splicing Cold War romance, *The Water-castle* (1964). From here, she plots her world along a deepening south-easterly axis to the Argo-Saronic island of Ídhra, onto which she maps her spiritually thirsty and psychologically brittle self in *A Rope of Vines* (1965). A Greece both enthralling and pitiless is also the inspiration for the archipelagic aggregations of rock- and island-forms, set against maplike gridlines, that are placed in challenging dialogue with pared-down poetic utterances in *Poems with Drawings* (1969).

And then there is Chamberlain's last major completed creative venture, the play *The Protagonists*: conceived in 1967, performed in 1968 and published here for the first time. It is a work to which her whole oeuvre can be said to gather. At first, it may seem a rupture in her career. But it would be a mistake to regard its form, its visceral response to a particular event, and the challenge its obscenities, ironies and totalitarian officialese pose to Chamberlain's 'default' lyricism as a wholly new departure. *The Protagonists* emerges from a career-long analysis of the freedoms and incarcerations – grand and petty, creative and social – that Brenda Chamberlain negotiated as an artist-writer, and as a woman. Far more knowingly than has been realised, her work had from the 1940s mapped her shifting identities (gender, sexual, cultural, spiritual and creative, all permanently under pressure) onto various physical landscapes. *The Protagonists* continues that autobiographical project. Located at the interface of the classical, Epic and absurdist traditions, the play is a profoundly confessional as well as a political cry.

Welsh Hellenism

Surprisingly early, a 'fatal' Greece became the loadstone of Brenda Chamberlain's island imagination. She was to emphasise that during her time on Bardsey (as a permanent resident from 1947 to 1957, then as a summer sojourner until the early 1960s), 'the mediterranean washed [her] dreams'.[4]

Developed in the poetry and early prose portraits of Bardsey in the late 1940s (following the breakdown of her marriage to John Petts) is an uncanny brand of Welsh Hellenism, a Welsh-Greek mythos. Chamberlain's geographical imagination was powerfully pre-modern in that she conceived of the western Celtic seaboard as vitally connected, physically and culturally, to the Mediterranean, where 'the Welsh sea' joins 'its fountain-head, the maternal middle ocean that hisses round promontories of pale-boned islands'.[5] A manuscript prose fragment written, it seems, just before she left Bardsey, configures the Mediterranean (in an echo of the aching Keats) as the 'bright South'. Drenched with Hellenic fatalism, *Tide-race* subtly charts the gravitational pull of Greece; 'wine-dark' and 'Odyssean', the Welsh sea around Bardsey is experienced in *Tide-race* as Homeric, and the archetypal Chamberlainian figure of the keening, fated female watcher is a classicisation of her own Welsh-Irish self. Of the sea-poems in the first part of her 1958 volume of poetry, *The Green Heart*, the *Hudson Review* commented: 'her Welsh fishing villages have a Mediterranean quality about them; the Furies, the Sirens, are about to appear . . . these are the Aegean islands and these the archaic fishermen of Homer'. P.N. Furbank in *Time and Tide* referred to the poems' 'Delphic bareness'. In *Tide-race*, the reviewer for the *Manchester Evening News* saw the 'almost Mediterranean colouring' of a Welsh world 'that, in other eyes, might seem all greens and greys'.[6] H.J. Fleure's Aegean ethnography of the Welsh, plotted in 1939 in the pages of *Wales*[7] in such a way as to make Wales seem 'a sort of island' (as Linda Adams has noted), bolstered the sense of Welsh culture as an outflow of a transfusive Aegean.[8] Synge spoke of the 'Greek kinship' of the tales he heard on Aran;[9] likewise, Chamberlain recognised in Welsh myth a tragic, theatrical, fatalistic note – the very note she strikes at the beginning of *Tide-race*, with what is in effect a *dramatis personae*. She sounds it again at the end of the book, as epitaphic metacommentary (reminiscent of a Greek chorus) merges with the 'alienated' awareness characteristic of absurdist theatre. The accents of *The Protagonists* are already here:

> A little larger than life, dancing with more abandon and grotesqueness than the others; with the devil nudging his elbow and manipulating a wire in his head, is [Cadwaladr] . . . On this small stage, this microcosm, in the middle of a scene, the shadow of death falls on the players.[10]

Chamberlain first visited Greece in 1962 with a male companion (the relationship with her partner on Bardsey, Jean van der Bijl, having come to an end). The 1960s marked a period of emotional loneliness for her, played out along that axis linking Wales and Greece. In her 1962 journal (a portion of which was published in *Mabon*),[11] she maps her journey through Germany and Italy to Greece. The tense trip was the occasion of frank self-analysis (a Greek tragic *anagnorisis*, or process of recognition, as she might have conceived of it): she speaks of herself as a 'simpleton', walking blindly 'into traps'.[12] And yet: 'I hate to be thought of as sweet and gentle – I'm bloody-minded and obstinate and terribly sad and seething-wild underneath'.[13] Travelling down the boot of Italy, she feels Greece exerting its pressure on her. And then she enters Hellenic waters, the fateful sea; Wales is summoned in another of her trademark 'communication[s] across "deep water"':

> The mainland of Greece – a dolphin leapt! Homesick for my own island at sight of the first small fishing-boats passing us, the men standing as they do in the Enlli [Bardsey] boats, easily balanced and full of pride. It seems unbelievable to be entering Greek waters . . .[14]

She was to mine this journal for the opening of *A Rope of Vines*, as she was to mine a later journal for the burdened utterances of *The Protagonists*. Her first impressions of mainland Greece immediately went beyond the superficially touristic; indeed, her work from this point forward sets out to contest touristic constructions of a welcoming, sun-drenched, recreational Greece. *The Protagonists* was mercilessly to unmask and parody such 'outsiderly' rhetoric. Chamberlainian Greece – as she would emphasise in *A Rope of Vines* – is an 'uneasy' place, both known and alien: 'I had dreamed of a classical Greece, but in fact, this is already the East' (*RoV*, p. 24).

October 1962 sees Chamberlain admiring '[h]ip-swinging girls' and '[m]en like brigands' in 'that prevalent red blood-shot light'. Her superstitious bent invests natural and built landscapes with a disturbing fatalism, a tragic inevitability; 'Sybil-cats' prowl over the 'classic marbles' of the Parthenon above Athens; another cat 'declaim[s] from one of the Tragedies, in the most perfect Greek, somewhere under [her] window in the well of the courtyard'.[15] Viewed in the light of these descriptions, the car crash in mid-October 1962 in which Chamberlain and her partner were involved (with her 'superstitions and fetishes and myths', she was convinced the 'le Baux cross' she wore had saved her life) has the force of a predestined event in the dramatic arc of the trip. Greece is both bewitching and threatening: 'Night near Patras, roaring of the wind-tunnel of trees, the moon (diseased)[,] the sky (red)[,] thunder and lightning. Suffocating heat. A feeling of danger'.[16] Greece is crux and contradiction: empowering and emancipating on the one hand, deathly and annihilating on the other. Both *A Rope of Vines* and *The Protagonists* were to analyse, if not resolve, the paradox. In a journal entry that *The Protagonists* would ironise and render tragic, Chamberlain sees 'a square, archaic woman dressed in black', striding with 'superb confidence' through Athens:

> If you want to savour freedom, walk down any
> road in Greece and look at the faces, the way of
> walking of these people.[17]

And in another entry that would soon become a distressful reminder of past freedoms, Chamberlain writes on the ferryboat, the *Appia*:

> How wonderful, to be in a free world, that is, able
> to take out my notebook anywhere and at any
> time and write freely. No suspicious eyes (I have
> been told my notebook would be suspect in Jugo-
> Slavia[)]. Sitting on the dry part of the locker,
> staring at the rain-speckled sea, or standing
> braced, as the ship cuts into the open sea-swell.
> Blue-red waters, full of sponges and squid,
> antique vases and bronze limbs.[18]

That word, 'braced', would return in *The Protagonists* to describe the stance, not of the exhilarated passenger tossed on the living, unshackled Greek sea, but of political prisoners – tense, defensive, on the stretch, anticipating acts of violence (see p. 16). Even the journal entry quoted above is fraught with fatality in its closing reminder of a civilization's *disjecta membra*. Similarly: 'Warm-fleshed marble [pillars] organic as trees, human-veined. Sit a moment on a rock – a grave-chill strikes the bone'. That deathful contact with the ground of Greece elicits from Chamberlain 'A compulsion to cry like a wolf, overcome by the menace of the sky and the ferocity of the sun; to confess I am less than the sand sifted on the marble steps, I am nothing[,] nothing, I want no identity.'[19] And yet, this first landfall inspired in her a desire to write 'heroic' verse, which implies a 'public' mode – a poetry that would take as its subject aspects of national struggle through time:

Leaning on the ship's rail, in the warm drizzle, how I want to write poetry, but I've at last faced the fact that my prose is better . . . I want to write heroic stuff like the modern Greek poets produce, to bring Time together, time past and present.[20]

That 'heroic' project, radically revised in the context of grim political realities, would five years later find a form in drama. Despite her statement in the 1962 journal that she would have preferred to view the Parthenon 'without the flood-lighting, which simply made a stage-set' out of an icon that 'does not need to be dramatised',[21] she would feel compelled to make a stage-set of Greece.

'Unrelenting Struggle': Ídhra

Soon the opportunity arose for Chamberlain to spend an extended period on the Argo-Saronic island of Ídhra, separated from the Peloponnese peninsula by a slender sound (less treacherous than that between Llŷn and Bardsey), in a house belonging to the daughter of a friend. Fittingly, the man with whom she had first visited Bardsey island in 1946, Henry Michalski, also had a house on Ídhra.[22] As Chamberlain later recalled, a stay during the summer and autumn of 1963 (which coincided with a Welsh Arts Council peripatetic exhibition of her most distinguished artistic work to date, alongside that of Ernest Zobole), became a residence (punctuated by return trips to Bangor) that lasted until late 1967. '[C]learly an outsider, if not quite a tourist' (in Anthony Conran's formulation),[23] she was part of an international artistic and literary 'colony' on the island (Leonard Cohen was there), though it is clear there was a measure of assimilation within the native communities of Ídhra port, the 'Kala Pigadhia' (or 'Good Wells'), and the convent of Agia Efpraxia, 500 metres above the port on the flank of Mount Eros. 'Greece offers you something harder – the discovery of yourself', Lawrence Durrell wrote in his account of his residence on Corfu, *Prospero's Cell* (1945) – a major influence on both the form and the focus of Chamberlain's *A Rope of Vines*.[24] Chamberlain's book is cast in the form of a 'journal' of numbered sections. An expressive object, it carries her own line drawings that supplement (and dislocate) the text, and is designed with wide white spaces around the 'islands' of the text, conjuring the bleaching light of the gulf. Proclaiming a spiritual 'surfacing' from the submarine territory of Bardsey into the 'nourishing' light of 'the mittelmeer' (*RoV*, p. 15), the book is a haunting analysis of the competing claims of various island selves, a meditation on being 'cell-enclosed' – on islands, in whitewashed monastery cells, and in the flesh: 'I, you, each in a separate cell, a cocoon of self, which we cannot disown or creep from, or break, or exchange for another' (*RoV*, p. 97). Here again, the language and confined geographies of *The Protagonists* are taking shape.

Beginning with the death of an English tourist and the incarceration of the writer's friend, 'Leonidas', for manslaughter, *A Rope of Vines* charts the various forms – meteorological, psychological – in which the 'iron-bound savage island, Ydra-shale', gradually takes on 'a sense of nightmare unreality' (*RoV*, p. 141) in excoriating Aegean light. There is something epitaphic about each journal entry. *A Rope of Vines* is both intensely introspective and attuned to various local and national histories of violence; it ends amid fears of a 'police state' that reflect the profound instabilities of early-to-mid-decade Greek politics, precipitated by the 'fraudulent parliamentary election' of 1961, but reaching back to the Civil War of 1946–9, the Second World War, and General Ioannis Metaxas's 'August 4 Regime' of 1936. The final pages of *A Rope of Vines* subtly map Chamberlain's 'struggle between the flesh and the prayer-wheel' onto the famous 'Unrelenting Struggle' of Georgios Papandreou (1888–1968) and his EK (Centre Union) party against the governing right-wing ERE (National Radical Union) under Konstantinos Karamanlis and then Panagiotis Kanellopoulos.[25] The result of democratic 'mobilisation' from 1961 was victory for Papandreou in the elections of 1963 and 1964; for Chamberlain, the 'terror' of Ídhra at this time is a complex of emotional and environmental disturbance, political uncertainty and the threat of military violence in an uncanny atmosphere of 'half-suppressed festivity': 'the port is filled with Marines, with rifles at the ready. Marines with fixed bayonets outside the Library, Marines outside the Gymnasium, where the women are voting' (*RoV*, p. 135). Chamberlain chooses to end *A Rope of Vines* with a reflection on acts of self-invention in a world of talismanic external objects ('these enduring boats, laden with melons and water pots'). Bound up with such 'metacritical' observations are her recently articulated political fears regarding how those in power can, in turn, 'invent' us, rendering us 'fictions' that harden, terrifyingly and absurdly, into reality:

> I am afraid of the police-state, of ships with loudspeakers that come to tell the people the way they shall vote, I am made afraid by the fear of the people . . . We were peaceably eating our dinners at Graphos'. Two policemen came in, one behind the other. For whom were they looking? We were the guilty, we were ready to be led away and to be interrogated. We were guilty because we dared to be individuals, to be free to walk about. He flushed, the man at the next table, frowning in concentration at his plate. He hoped the policeman would not see how his hands were shaking. He was on bail, we were, every one of us, on bail for nameless crimes. (*RoV*, p. 154)

The paragraph's folded discourse and collapsed perspectives enact the very incarceration that is condemned: the entrance of the policemen, as onto a stage, results in a series of *self-denunciations*: 'We were the guilty'. Those loudspeakers and edicts, the police double-act, the reflections on doomed individualism and the 'case-study' of the physical responses of the subject 'at the next table' all anticipate the shocking world of *The Protagonists*.

Towards Eclipse: 1966

Returning to Ídhra in May 1964 following a period in Bangor, Chamberlain began a fascinating collaboration with the dancer Robertos Saragas (1927–79), whose fluid movements she drew. Back in London at the Lamda Theatre in November of the same year, Chamberlain, Saragas and Nahami Abbell (American student of the pioneering German expressionist dancer and choreographer, Mary Wigman) came together to stage a 'dance recital' in which the actress Dorothy Tutin recited Chamberlain's poems. Examining Chamberlain's papers in the National Library of Wales, one comes across delicate, sinuous drawings of Saragas's form in stylised motion; they are a delighted articulation of freedom, but also an inscription of the fear of seeing such vibrant creative expression proscribed.[26]

Papandreou's government held power – most uneasily – from early 1964 until the summer of 1965. Reforms instituted by his party, together with moves to guarantee greater civil liberty, gave some reason for hope, though the administration was always a brittle affair owing to the government's attempts to control the military (in particular the officer corps) and the increasing rift between Papandreou and King Constantine. Stable parliamentary government was deeply compromised. The *Iouliana* or 'July events' (also known as the 'Apostasy' or 'Royal Coup') of 1965 saw Papandreou sacked as Prime Minister by the king and a number of short-lived interim administrations formed against a background of 'economic militance' and civil unrest that resulted in several deaths.[27] Witnessing the breakdown of stable government, elements of the military Right began to plot. The desperate political uncertainties of 1965–6 were paralleled by Brenda Chamberlain's emotional and psychological brittleness.

The pen drawings prepared on Ídhra for *A Rope of Vines* are characterised by a starker line than those in *Tide-race*, as Chamberlain worked towards a more epitaphic and desolate art as a vehicle for self-dissection. A series of ten disquieting graphic works created in 1965 on Ídhra, entitled 'The Black Bride', hints at an inner life of phobia and fear. Maurice Cooke suggests that the series

> has little connection with the island but must relate
> to some incident in [Chamberlain's] personal life,
> probably to a love affair, possibly to the hope and
> fear of a second marriage.[28]

Central to the series is the concept of female confinement and inter(n)ment. The 'bride' is 'in rigid profile, still and sometimes stiff as though held by enchantment'. The bride's blackness, Cooke hazards, 'hides the secret which is the bait for desire, and hides her own secret desire which is mixed with fear'. A surrounding form, suggestive of a veil, begins to enfold the bride; Chamberlain's notes (inscribed on the pictures) catch her in various attitudes of incarceration: 'La femme en Cage'; 'She is entombed'; 'The Bride is enmeshed'; 'Anonymous in a fishing net'; 'The black woman in a white shell'; 'The Bride enters the Sepulchre'.[29] She is also 'Blodeuwedd Fach' – the fated woman conjured from flowers as a wife for Lleu Llaw Gyffes in the fourth branch of the *Mabinogi* (a 'ruthless legend' that had haunted Chamberlain since at least the 1940s, and which had served as a powerful vehicle of her self-mythologisation).[30] The 'Black Bride' series is an enigmatic, layered work; the fact that the earliest image in the sequence is 'demonstrably a self-portrait'[31] strongly suggests the confessional import of the recurring trammels of cages, nets and tombs. The stark presence of six cages on the stage of *The Protagonists* at the end of 1968 would emphasise the continuity between the concerns of the play and the 'private' images of the 'Black Bride' series.

Chamberlain's remarkably candid Ídhra journal of 1966, entitled 'A Total Eclipse of the Sun', contains some of the most brutally confessional writing by a Welsh author. It bespeaks a need to log and externalise inner turmoil, to plot her own identity vis-à-vis the dysfunctional 'colony' on Ídhra, and to map her condition in relation to the natural environment. The January and February portions of the journal were published posthumously in *Mabon*.[32] The evidence of the first and second drafts of the journal suggests that it was written with an eventual audience in mind, but this does not render disingenuous its bitter, distressful accounts of the self. Everything Chamberlain wrote was an exercise in elasticising the boundaries that traditionally separate life writing and fiction, in gaining purchase on changing identities by defamiliarising them and rendering them relational. Following the journal's Cassandra-like epigraph –

> It is the end of our time. These are the last months,
> weeks, perhaps days, that we shall be free to sit in
> the sun. A terrible change is about to take place. It
> has been foretold.[33]

– is an epitaph manqué that shares something of the prophetic energies of the epigraph:

I could, I should destroy myself, from the roof into
the almond tree, on the black night wind while the
drum still beats to overlay the sound of my fall.[34]

The gathering political storm, both in Greece and globally, was
more than some objective correlative of Chamberlain's inner
disturbances; it was emphatically part of that psychological
destabilisation. As she wrote in her journal in early July 1966:

Dinner beneath the house-vine under a field of stars
– in the shadow of war – Cyprus, Turkey, Vietnam.
From somewhere, to gain enough strength to
shore up the walls against flood.[35]

The journal tracks the island communities' networks of
suspicion and its seemingly endemic unhealthfulness: the
'plain-clothes Dick' shadowing elements of the expatriate
colony (narcotics being the quarry); dark thoughts of
incarceration and ironic (and not-so-ironic) reflections on
how that experience might serve as a creative spur ('They say
Harkness (prison-cropped) sleeps on the floor of [his] cell with
two murderers. Perhaps, after this experience, he will write
something worthwhile, perhaps not'); a disquieting knock at
the door that heralds the entry of an armed man who uses
Chamberlain's hall as a shortcut; mental conflicts ('The South
African writer of pornography is looking dangerously mad;
[h]unched shoulders, one eye looking out (glazed)[,] the other
looking inward (fixed)'; the story of the 'girl friend' of Katerina
('a young poet from Athens'), who collapses on the Good Wells
from 'an overdose of nerve pills'; and others' coded cries for
help: '[He said:] "My friend woke up this morning with a desire
to kill himself.["] "My friend" was of course, himself'.[36] Clearly,
the early months of 1966 saw Chamberlain deeply involved in
others' mental pain: 'Why did I not study psychiatry, then I

should have been paid for listening'.[37] Her accounts of others' tragedies were to prove uncanny self-portraits.

The Ídhra of the 1966 journal is an island of death, pain, hysteria and apprehension. This most intimate of Chamberlainian chronicles is shot through with meditations on death, sex, and emotional isolation in a supercharged atmosphere leading up to the total eclipse of the sun on 20 May 1966 – an event described in an entry that is a tour de force of fabling observation:

> The earth gradually bleached. Through smoked glass and sunglasses we peered into a bowl of water at the burning sun. Best, was through a folded pad of exposed film. As shadows moved from left to right, coldness came, & a body-lightness. Shadows of foliage surreal, sun-moonlight. Intensity of cypress-tree green. Very cold. We were on the roof, separated from one another by a small zone of iciness; stars were faintly visible. Our shadows shortened, became more precise. The neighbours were indoors, there was no sound from dog or donkey. As the shade passed and life returned to our world, firerockets soared up from the port – the life-giver had returned.[38]

The account gathers to itself the journal's preoccupations with deathliness, shadow-life, shifting identities, creativity, fleshly proximity and the influence of wider cosmic forces. Clearly party to others' inner turmoil, Chamberlain was also wrestling with her own demons. A haunting pathology of landscape is among the most disturbing imaginative achievements of the journal. Poetically calibrated botanical lists pulse throughout the work: 'There are deep purple vetches glowing out of the yellow-blooming gorse, palest lemon vetches, ven[e]tian red vetches, and other flowers so exquisite[,] small, fragile, one can scarcely believe they have power to break earth so stubborn'.[39] These are countermanded by darker botanies of the spirit: 'A scent of roses and of bile'; 'soil bright as blood outside the door'; 'Asphodels, tall as saplings, translucent in the sun, have the white faces of little dead novices'.[40] As *A Rope of Vines* records, Chamberlain went on a brief 'retreat' to the convent of Agia Efpraxia; there in the whitewashed cell she found both spiritual serenity and a sharpened apprehension of incarceration. She makes a point of noting the nuns' mode of addressing her:

> To Ephpraxia where, greatly welcoming, the
> nuns referred to me as 'the unfortunate Brenda',
> a superstitious endearment to keep the evil eye
> away from one. Scylla, myrrh, wild lavender.[41]

The talismanic flower list is itself a personal mantra against 'the evil eye'; properly scilla (a genus of blue-flowering herb), Chamberlain's 'Scylla' is a Freudian slip that summons the sea monster of *The Odyssey* from the depths of the unconscious.

Profound depression overwhelmed her, as did an all-consuming 'lassitude' following periods of creative endeavour.[42] 'To feel ashamed of the blackness of one's moods', she notes, 'helps not at all'. Feeling that she 'lag[ged] behind the days, in the past of that other island', Bardsey, her mind turned to the 'luxury' of being 'put away' in an asylum.[43] The voice of a woman desperately seeking to persuade herself of her own emotional resources and wells of reciprocity is to the fore in entries whose poetic expressiveness is a function of the fear of losing that capacity for response: 'I can love and love (again I can) with south wind of springtime, south wind of love, almonds fresh to the taste and touch'.[44] In March she suddenly encounters in a steep, narrow lane the funeral cortège of an old woman, 'hands tied together, mouth stuffed with cotton wool'. So precariously balanced is the coffin that Chamberlain imagines the possibility of the corpse pitching up towards her. In July, during the burial of another old woman, she configures herself uncannily as the embryonic dead, lying 'in the shuttered womb' with bells tolling and mourners weeping.[45] Accounts of recurring 'anxiety nightmares'; fantasies of being consigned, like Eurydice, to the Shades after a period of struggling towards the light; and images of the groping hands of blind beggars conspire to invest an image such as that of a canary 'throw[ing] itself against the bars' of the cage on Chamberlain's outside wall with a personal symbolic charge.[46] In one unsettling March entry, she aligns her own case history and that of a fellow islander with the experience of an individual whose schizophrenic breakdown she had witnessed, terrifyingly first hand, in the tormented first week of January 1959 on Bardsey:

> [The unnamed acquaintance on Ídhra] is sure he is
> becoming mad. An unconscious desire like mine
> and Panek's on Enlli, to get away from intolerable
> circumstances?[47]

'Panek' is Berthold (Bert) Panĕk, a displaced Pole who arrived in Britain after the Second World War, tormented (it seems) by some terrible guilt related to the War and to women. He had sought a life of prayer in various European monasteries, but had been rejected; in 1956 the tenancy of Plas Bach on Bardsey offered the chance of healing. By January 1959 he had succumbed to terrible mental dislocation; as *Tide-race* records, he was gabbling sections of the Roman Catholic Mass, believing he was assailed by devils.[48] However different her own clinical condition, Chamberlain movingly acknowledges a pathological lineage as she summons the hermit of Bardsey to Ídhra in the spring of 1966.

This extended profile of the 1966 journal is necessary since Chamberlain draws on its stark confessionality to create the psychological and emotional world of *The Protagonists*, which clearly emerges from both a political and a personal crisis. Moreover, the journal sees Chamberlain experiment with sardonic tonalities that would soon constitute one of the major discourses of *The Protagonists*, in such entries as: 'Artist, poor dab, passionately embracing his canvas (painted sex) forgets his wife's a whore'. At the very end of the journal, there is also, tellingly, a brief foray into drama; eavesdropping on quayside exchanges, Chamberlain was beginning to sound out the directness – and ironic indirection – of speech:

> Chef de Police to X[:] 'X, you are accused of the attempted rape of a girl-child; the same of a boy-child.'
> X. 'If I paint your portrait in oils, will you forget my mistakes?'
> Chef de Police: 'I shall start sitting for my portrait tomorrow morning'.[50]

Tracing the entries from the journal in *The Protagonists* reveals the play's intimate personal genetics and maps the imbrication of the political catastrophe Chamberlain felt was imminent and her own mental and emotional predicament. As the Notes in this edition show, portions of the journal are incorporated bodily into the play; they are assigned not only to the single female character, L, with her terrible history of loss, but also to the male characters in the play's shifting matrix of power. The 1966 journal is also powerfully present through allusion, in the play's studied enhancement of the theme of madness and in the stark literalisation (now in a specific political context) of the focal Chamberlainian experience of the 1960s: island incarceration.

April Coup: 'Shot on Sight'

Chamberlain returned home to Bangor in December 1966, the month in which the two main party leaders in Greece, Papandreou and Kanellopoulos, agreed with the king that a general election be held 'not later than May 1967'.[51] A cadre of colonels was now plotting in earnest. As David Close notes, 'The electoral result that was generally expected was a large majority for Papandreou, which would humiliate the King and threaten the military conspirators' jobs'.[52] During the winter of 1966–7, it seems Chamberlain had decided to return permanently to Ídhra. Alan McPherson – at that time a Philosophy undergraduate at Bangor, who would play the part of the Guard in the October 1968 performances of *The Protagonists* – recalls meeting Chamberlain in the spring of 1967 'at a leaving party held for her in Upper Bangor'.[53] She arrived back on the island three days before the Colonels' coup d'état of 21 April 1967.

Tanks 'rolled through the streets of Athens', entered Syntagma Square and 'trained their weapons on the Parliament'.[54] The conspirators, led by Colonel Georgios Papadopoulos, had 'made their preparations with thoroughness born of long experience'.[55] As Thanos Veremis notes, these middle-ranking soldiers 'had come of age during the Civil War period', and their mentality harked back to that period.[56] The king – the military's pawn – could do nothing. The putsch was swift and ruthlessly effective; a 'puppet government' was appointed, but the reins of power were held by Papadopoulos. The Junta would last until 1974; Chamberlain would not live to see the restoration of parliamentary democracy in Greece. Given the strategic geopolitical importance of Greece as a bulwark against the Soviet threat and the shifting balance of power in the eastern Mediterranean following the Arab-Israeli Six-day War in June 1967, the Americans 'were not slow in reconciling themselves to the new regime'.[57] For its part, the UK government under

Harold Wilson, aware of the complexities of British military and economic 'interests' in Greece and the Mediterranean, was slow to register its unease, and did so eventually only euphemistically.[58] Following the coup, political undesirables were rounded up and placed under house arrest, imprisoned, or exiled to detention centres on Greek islands. The country became an archipelago of prison isles. The Colonels took control of every aspect of Greek public life, from the armed forces and judiciary to education and the Church. Needless to say, freedom of the press was suspended, and a wider programme of censorship instituted. Any activity smacking of leftism, broadly defined, was regarded as suspicious; networks of surveillance were reestablished. Greece became a Police State. The regime certainly deployed torture, which in certain cases resulted in death.[59]

The ideology of the Junta was as unsophisticated as its methods were brutal. Claiming to have intervened in order to preserve the 'Helleno-Christian state' from a communist plot and from 'Western neo-anarchism',[60] and alleging the Dictatorship was merely a necessary 'parenthesis', it bombarded the population with crass essentialist slogans 'about country, religion, family and communist iniquities'. These were voiced, printed, and marked on blue-and-white boards across Greece:[61] 'The revolution, carried out bloodlessly, marches forward to fulfilment of its manifest destiny'; 'Communists are traitors to the nation'.[62] Some of the Junta's edicts plumbed the depths of absurdity; long hair, beards and miniskirts were proscribed as marks of western decadence and 'moral decline' (the decree against them was 'hastily rescinded in the interests of Greece's vital tourist trade'), while the music of both The Beatles and the celebrated left-wing deputy, Mikis Theodorakis, was also banned as 'anti-ethnic'.[63] Assessing the banalities of the Junta, Richard Clogg in 1972 identified facile 'verbiage' and 'what the novelist George Theotokas diagnosed as . . . ancestoritis' as two of the main characteristics of the regime's 'pseudo-ideology' and 'ultra-nationalist' rhetoric.[64] Papadopoulos began to deploy a pathological discourse that identified the Greek nation as a bound 'sick body' that required urgent intervention if 'health' was to be regained: 'The restraints [imposed by the regime] are the straps that fasten the patient to the operating table so that he may go through the surgery devoid of any danger'.[65]

The response of Greek writers and artists to the Junta's programme of pre-censorship, censorship, library purges and incarceration (as Rodis Roufos notes, it was imaginative writing, social science research, theatre and cinema 'that suffered most') was a principled silence, a 'spontaneous, silent strike'.[66] Although 1969 was to mark a change in writers' willingness to test the limits of censorship and engage in explicit denunciations (the poet and Nobel laureate Giorgos Seferis's famous statement on the BBC World Service in March of that year was a famous watershed), the creative arts remained fatally hobbled until the regime collapsed in 1974. As Karen van Dyck argues, what Papadopoulos sought was control over meaning itself, a 'mimetic relationship between *what one said and what one meant*'. His 'ongoing attempt to drain language of its figural force' was evident

> in his press law, which included the ludicrous mandate that all books bear titles corresponding to their contents. In a similar vein, all major newspapers were ordered to carry identical front-page stories. Such actions reveal his unease with semantic instability. Like some latter-day Cratylus arguing for a 'fitness of signs', Papadopoulos wanted the word and the thing to be exactly the same.[67]

Writers and publishers responded to this self-defeating attempt to render language transparently denotative by deploying the creative and material tools of their trade. Newspaper editors printed the regime's 'mandatory statements' and edicts 'in the same type and format as obituaries' – a brilliant stroke that not only foregrounded the deathliness of the Junta's totalitarian pronouncements, but also ensured the regime was forever announcing its own death. Writers also had recourse to ludic layouts, parodic typography, homophonic puns and deliberate spelling errors that registered 'subversive messages'.[68] Brenda Chamberlain was clearly aware of such acts of writerly resistance; *The Protagonists* was to make full use of the instabilities of language as a strategy of protest.

Chamberlain recalled her own immediate response to the coup in an interview with Alan McPherson in the University College of North Wales, Bangor student newspaper – *Forecast* – in May 1968. She remembers an 'uncanny total negativeness', an eerie silence punctuated by the 'hourly bulletins' and edicts received on café transistors:

> everything was, 'If you do this, SHOT ON SIGHT.' 'If you do that you'll be SHOT ON SIGHT.' And it was everything, so that nothing could happen, you see.[69]

Although she was not herself harassed by the police, she recalls the feeling of being 'reassessed' as an outsider. Aware of the presence of an 'informer' in Ídhra port, she was conscious of the need 'to keep as quiet as possible and definitely not to talk publicly'. In a BBC Radio 4 Wales *Spectrum* interview with William Tydeman, broadcast on 4 April 1968, she was to refer to the paralysing 'perfection' of the coup – 'so classic in its working, so perfectly machined'.[70] In the year of her death, she would emphasise that a pall descended on the creative imagination – 'I waited for something to happen to me, or in me' – and that from spring to autumn 1967 she found it 'impossible to paint or write'.[71]

Remarkably, it was in this atmosphere that Chamberlain visited the detention island of Léros in the Dodecanese, close to the Turkish coast, traditionally the site of state prisons and sanatoria.[72] How this was achieved is not clear. By the summer of 1967, two camps had been established there – at Parthéni in the north, and at Lakki in the south. Chamberlain plainly states in the *Spectrum* interview that she travelled twice to the island, in May and August 1967. During the earlier visit, she noted the 'tremendous number of police' there; by the time of the second trip, Léros had become a fully-fledged detention island – a 'nightmare'. Seeing 'lorryloads of police parked on the road', she imagined them 'sitting in the trees, thick as locusts'. That image of a plague of totalitarian predators would find its way into *The Protagonists*: 'Out there among the leaves of the shade-tree the secret police sit thick as locusts, munching our reputations' (p. 10). Chamberlain's account of her visits accords with the facts: deportations to Léros began in earnest in July 1967, with the arrival of '200 prominent leftists, including pro-communist deputies', who were housed in 'the buildings of an Italian wartime naval base', 'expanded and converted into an exile camp', as *The Times* reported.[73] In early September they were joined by 2000 prisoners from another detention island, Gyaros (known also as Gioura) in the northern Cyclades; among them was the distinguished poet and activist, Yiannis Ritsos (an appeal for his release was signed in September 1968 by 'poets, publishers and literary agents' including Hugh McDiarmid, Ted Hughes, and Stephen Spender).[74] By April 1968, '[s]igned statements alleging conditions of "inhuman isolation and moral torture"' were being smuggled out of the camp at Parthéni.[75] The International Red Cross struggled to gain full access to the camps. Conditions were 'not suitable for prolonged detention' and illness was rife; in 1970, an appeal from Léros declared: 'Death is lurking in each ward, each bed'.[76]

The 1968 interview in *Forecast* reveals that, following the coup, Chamberlain began to jot down 'small statements' and record 'fragments' of speech overheard on post-coup Ídhra. She was amassing the living data of everyday discourse, waiting for it to find its form. That store of speech was supplemented during her second visit to Léros in August. There was never any initial intention of forging a dramatic work from this exercise in eavesdropping, which one might regard as Chamberlain's creative challenge to official surveillance. 'You'd never written a play before?' Alan McPherson asked in the *Forecast* interview; 'I never thought of using that form, never', replied Chamberlain, adding that she had contemplated film as a form, 'but never a play'. It was the intervention of an American friend on Ídhra (who was himself writing a play) that convinced Chamberlain that the material she had gathered was the stuff of a dramatic work:

> he read these fragments and said, 'My God! How strong; this is a play!' . . . it was as though a key had been turned on something. I just saw the whole thing come . . . At eight o'clock every morning I just sat and put it down – it came so fast that I always had one of those little books, these little Greek notebook things, and when I went down into the port or anywhere, I had one of these with me . . . People were speaking – it was direct speech. I never wrote any happenings, any direct description; it just happened through their voices. It was terribly exciting . . . I was checking back all the time, seeing if they were speaking out of character, but they were always themselves, you know; I thought it can't be true that this person is saying this, but it always keyed in in a strange way.[77]

Used to composing prose and poetry with 'painful slowness', Chamberlain felt this new process of 'listening in' (as William Tydeman called it) wholly liberating.

The Greek family with whom she was living knew she was writing a play, but Chamberlain was anxious not to implicate them in any way. She recalled that they 'looked over her shoulder' and saw the 'caged figures' she had drawn in order to visualise the positions of the actors on stage at key junctures (Figure 1);[78] the dialogue itself, however, 'meant nothing to them'. Advised by a friend not to speak of the play, or of the two visits to Léros (such was the suspicion in which resident 'aliens', internal movement and the creative act itself were held), Chamberlain replied: 'Well, I'll just say there were lovely flowers there'.[79] That said, she read *The Protagonists* to six friends whom she 'trusted absolutely'. On finishing the play, fuelled by retsina, she 'started reading from it at the top of [her] voice' in the company of old friends at a taverna. It was, she said 'a breaking out'.[80] She describes as 'violent' the response of two friends to the play's obsessive reflection on passports and identification; significantly, both friends were experiencing 'visa trouble'. The typescripts of the play are dated October– November 1967; it was written, Chamberlain insisted, 'at white-heat in three weeks'.[81] A drawing in the second draft of the play shows the view from her window above the line 'In this room, The Protagonists was written, Autumn 1967' (Figure 2). The completion of the play that autumn must have been one of the principal factors in Chamberlain's decision to return to Wales in December 1967.[82] *The Protagonists* clandestinely crossed policed borders: two copies of the dissident text were sent 'out through Cyprus'; Chamberlain carried another copy 'openly' in her shoulder bag, since she feared – rightly, as it turned out – that her suitcase would be searched.

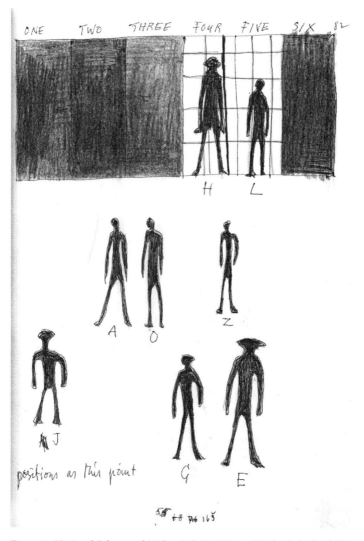

Figure 1: National Library of Wales, MS 21493D, p. 82 (third draft of *The Protagonists*). Chamberlain's drawing of the actors' 'positions a[t] this point' (i.e. O's line 'For once, I agree with you, maker of edicts'– see p. 35). Llyfrgell Genedlaethol Cymru/The National Library of Wales.

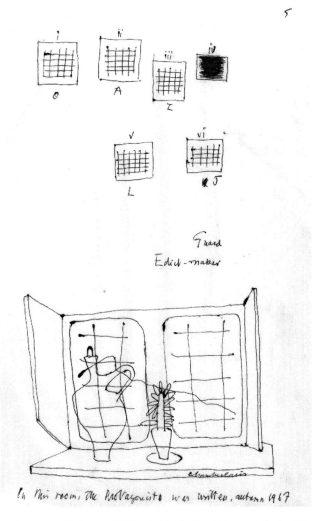

Figure 2: National Library of Wales, MS 21492D, p. 5 (second draft of *The Protagonists*). Chamberlain's drawing of the view from her window on Ídhra, between a sketch of the prisoners' cells at the beginning of the play and the statement 'In this room, The Protagonists was written, Autumn 1967'. Llyfrgell Genedlaethol Cymru/The National Library of Wales.

'Into the European Scene': The Bangor Archipelago

Alan McPherson smartly conceives of the Upper Bangor to which Chamberlain came 'home' (that concept now radically inflected) as a series of island spaces 'on the ridge' – in effect, a cultural archipelago.[83] Tony Conran's heroic figuring constructs these spaces as a series of 'courts' preserving 'the good ways'.[84] McPherson recalls Chamberlain 'erupting into [this] community' in the winter of 1967, 'a small, excitable refugee . . . fleeing an oppressive regime'.[85] She lodged first at 4 Menai View Terrace with the Mundle family, then in a flat at number 12 in the same row ('the only elegant terrace in the city . . . rather plain as Pevsner might put it, but handsome', as McPherson has it). The upper floors of number 12 were occupied by Cathrin Daniel – widow of the distinguished theologian, J. E. Daniel (President of Plaid Cymru, 1939–43) – and her family.[86] McPherson – by now a Philosophy postgraduate at Bangor – noted Chamberlain's characteristic itineraries as she 'bounced about Upper Bangor from one household to the next'.

Kate Holman notes that *The Protagonists* was sent to 'various organisations' at this time.[87] A copy went to Jeremy Brooks, Literary Manager of Peter Hall's Royal Shakespeare Company (and author of the novels *Jampot Smith* and *Smith, As Hero*). His response was encouraging (he promised to show the script to Trevor Nunn, the RSC's Artistic Director), even if the issue of the work's 'theatricality' gave him pause for thought. His assessment, sent in a letter to Chamberlain, was quoted in the programme leaflet printed for the first performance of the play (Figures 3a and 3b):

> A most distinguished and powerful piece of writing
> – a fully achieved work of art. Whether it is a play or
> not I don't yet know. You make your dramas more
> by a pattern of ideas than by a progression of actions

Figures 3a and 3b: programme leaflet for *The Protagonists*. Courtesy of Alan McPherson.

and the question must be whether that pattern is
strong enough to withstand the strain and degree of
loss that go with public performance.

Recognising, one might suggest, the heteroglossic effects
of *The Protagonists*, he proceeded in his original letter to
Chamberlain to compare the 'fusion of elements' in the
play with the work of that other writer-artist, David Jones.[88]
(Jones's cultural and linguistic syntheses are of course part
of a very different European literary project.) That Brooks's
appraisal appeared in the programme leaflet suggests that
Chamberlain recognised the validity of his calibration of the
play as a conceptually layered, generically plural and highly
stylised work that subordinates dramatic action to powerful
visual symbolism and the rhetoricity of speech.

Alan McPherson suspects that the first formal meeting that
brought together the personnel that would later crystallise
into *The Protagonists*' cast and production team was held in
Cathrin Daniel's lounge at 12 Menai View Terrace on 12 March
1968. McPherson's wife, Eirlys, and Anna Daniel took the
lead in organising the gathering; Chamberlain's schoolfriend
Joan Rees, the young professional actors John Owen Hughes
(Owen Garmon) and Gray Evans, and the actor and director
David Lyn were present, and possibly the professional Greek
actress Sophia Michopoulou, whom Chamberlain had recently
met in London. (Chamberlain emphasised how precisely
Michopoulou corresponded to the physical profile of L, the
character she would play in *The Protagonists*.) The Greek actress
was a member of Théatro Téchnis, the company led by Karolos
Koun, distinguished modern interpreter of classical Greek
drama and of the plays of Brecht, Pirandello and Ionesco.
According to the *North Wales Chronicle*, Michopoulou had left
Greece 'on a Russian ship', and was in September 1968 'unable
to reveal her full name', 'for fear of persecution when she

returns home'.[89] The group that had cohered around the project in early March must already have begun rehearsing passages from the play for the imminent BBC Radio 4 Wales interview with Chamberlain, broadcast in early April; a recording (by Alan McPherson) of a section of one of these rehearsals survives.[90] It is also likely that the 12 March gathering marked the inception of the Welsh Drama Studio, whose 'first essay' (as the *North Wales Chronicle* called it)[91] was to be *The Protagonists.*

Led by David Lyn, who had worked with the Royal Shakespeare Company and who was a member of the Welsh Theatre Company, The Welsh Drama Studio – a 'theatre workshop plan' – aimed 'to promote Welsh drama into the European scene'.[92] In September 1968, the *North Wales Chronicle* hazarded that the venture 'could be the beginning of a Welsh National Theatre in North Wales'. With Owen Garmon, Lyn had in 1966 performed in Cwmni Theatr Cymru's production of Gwenlyn Parry's play, *Saer Doliau* (Doll Doctor) whose absurdist credentials would have sharpened his awareness of the ways in *The Protagonists* locates itself in relation to the same tradition. Interviewed about the venture in September 1968 – his hair dyed 'a rich Teutonic gold' since he was playing the role of Karl, a 'German ex-prisoner of war', in *Lleifior*, a BBC adaptation of Islwyn Ffowc Elis's novel, *Cysgod y Cryman* (Shadow of the Sickle) – Lyn explained that the Welsh Drama Studio would serve as an engine for 'original plays' by Welsh authors who wished to 'try out their ideas'. Robustly, he stated that the venture would energise a culture enervated by what he saw as the 'Christmas carolling' of the Eisteddfod (*Saer Doliau*, premièred at the Aberafan Eisteddfod of 1966, was presumably the exception that proved the rule). At the same time, the Welsh Drama Studio would be part of a 'scene . . . as constructive and comprehensive and totally Welsh as the actors are'; it was not to be 'a theatre with Welsh accents'.[93] Lyn's aspiration asks us to take seriously the notion of *The*

Figure 4: Sophia Michopoulou (L) and Jeff Thompson (Z); September 1968 rehearsals. © Emyr Roberts.

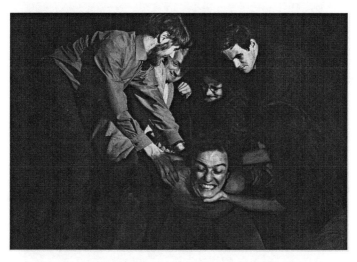

Figure 5: Around the central figure of Jeff Thompson (Z), from left: Gray Evans (O); David Lyn (Producer, standing in for Gwyn Parry, who played A); Alan McPherson (Guard); Vasilis Politis (H, head lowered); Owen Garmon (J); Sophia Michopoulou (L). September 1968 rehearsals. © Emyr Roberts.

Figure 6: Alan McPherson (Guard, left); Vasilis Politis (H). September 1968 rehearsals. © Emyr Roberts.

Figure 7: From left: Alan McPherson (Guard); Gray Evans (O); David Lyn (Producer); Owen Garmon (J). September 1968 rehearsals. © Emyr Roberts.

Protagonists as a piece of 'Welsh' theatre,[94] even as the play itself works hard to contest the very notion of art as a contribution to or expression of a *particular* 'national' life or ethnic experience.

By the spring of 1968 (that year of global protest), Chamberlain – remembered by McPherson as 'small, very active and intense' – was preparing not only for the production of *The Protagonists* (which had initially, and optimistically, been scheduled for June) but also for an exhibition of 'over 40 new works' at the Bangor Art Gallery. An article by Alan Twelves in the *North Wales Chronicle* emphasised the radical paring-down of Chamberlain's art that Greece had effected: he saw 'at once, a world of incredible complexity and outrageous simplicity' and noted Chamberlain's process of 'proposing, discarding and distilling' to achieve symbolic forms.[95] *The Protagonists* itself (a brief intervening account of which is offered by Twelves) and its staging by Lyn can usefully be considered as the product of a process of 'proposing, discarding and distilling' – a rejection of naturalistic representation in favour of stylised symbolisations of action and speech.

Rehearsals in the college's Prichard-Jones Hall, attended by Chamberlain,[96] were held throughout September and early October (see Figures 4–8), with the two performances, sponsored by the North Wales Association for the Arts, fixed for 11 and 12 October (a Friday and Saturday). In an undated note to McPherson, Chamberlain wrote: 'I was thrilled by what I saw last night at rehearsal. Thrilled, & terrified!'.[97] From the first, the cast and crew (described by Chamberlain in the *Spectrum* interview as a 'nucleus' of 'real enthusiasts') were clear that an orthodox stage would not be in tune with the demands (or political meanings) of a play that confronted the audience with six caged dissidents (A, L, J, O, Z and H, identified as subversives in a 'Black Dossier'),[98] and two representatives of the penal State in the shape of an 'Edict Maker' and a Guard (from whose belt hung a dead rabbit, dripping blood).[99] Robertos Saragas's lithe

Figure 8: Alan McPherson as the Guard; dress rehearsal, October 1968.

Figure 9 (right): 3-D reconstruction of the stage set for *The Protagonists* in Prichard-Jones Hall, University College of North Wales, Bangor, by Damian Walford Davies (Google SketchUp software), based on sketches in Katherine Elizabeth Holman, 'The Literary Achievement of Brenda Chamberlain' (unpublished MA thesis, University College of Swansea, 1976) and descriptions by Alan McPherson.

movements, joyfully drawn by Chamberlain on Ídhra, are here reduced to caged forms; Z's manic dances and his ungainly crawl, 'one leg raised and the other hopping, body arched to suggest deformity', are a grim parody of Saragasian freedom. Chamberlain explained that the Prichard-Jones hall should become 'Léros or any arid island', and that the play's action 'must be as close to the audience as possible – it should be in and around and among them – the audience should be around the cages so that they can begin to imagine that they are in the same situation'.[100] There would be no backdrops or scenery: 'the sense of background', of vistaed depth, Chamberlain emphasised, would be 'cut out'. Storeyed scaffolding, with the six prisoners' cages at stage level, dominated the apsidial end of the hall; the audience sat on three sides of a stage that consisted of the area in front of the scaffolding and a bridge or (a)isle, between two sunken areas, extending out to that section of the audience sitting in the apse (see Figure 9). That central seating area was gently raked, and so resembled a classical Greek theatre in miniature.[101] A black curtain hung behind the cages to obscure the length of the hall. McPherson describes the staging as 'intimate'.

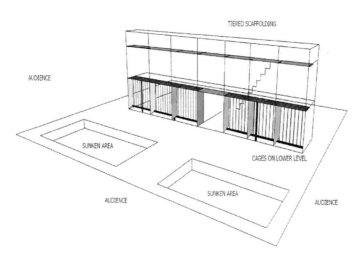

the welsh drama studio

sponsored by the north wales association
for the arts

presents

brenda
chamberlain's

THE PROTAGONISTS

directed by david lyn

in the prichard jones hall of the university college of north wales
bangor   caernarvonshire

friday 11th & saturday 12th october at 8p.m.

Figure 10: Publicity poster for *The Protagonists*. By kind permission of Emyr
Roberts.

Figure 11: Publicity poster for *The Protagonists*: detail of Chamberlain's
drawing-collage. By kind permission of Emyr Roberts.

The play's striking publicity poster (Figure 10) is itself a nuanced literary, artistic and political statement. It has the force of a flag, with a collage by Chamberlain in the upper left ('canton') space (the site of the cross in the Greek flag). Thus its very 'vexillological' (flaglike) design immediately raises the vexed issue of national(ist) symbologies. The drawing itself – by Chamberlain – is an Ídhra work. Cubist in style, it depicts an agglomeration of human bodies in various strained and straining poses on what appears to be a craft or raft, against a sky and sea of English and French newspaper cuttings (Figure 11). The central figures have disturbing cadaver-like faces. Behind the drawing, I suggest, is a disturbing template: Géricault's *The Raft of the Medusa* (painted 1818–19), in which dying victims of shipwreck – humanity *in extremis* – distressfully hail a passing ship from the floating island of their makeshift raft. Chamberlain's figures have clearly been arranged in such a way as to evoke the dying attitudes of Géricault's. Thus the poster is an ensign of crisis, a tragic banner – an ironised Greek flag that allusively identifies the *dramatis personae* of the play (and the 'nation' under the Junta) as an alienated community of 'castaways' on a sea of fractured world 'news'. Like the remnant on the Medusa's raft, they will turn on each other in their fear.

The stage manager, Joy Ostle (Joy Roberts in 1968), recalls a moving scene before the actors took the stage on the evening of the first performance. Chamberlain approached each member of the production, pressing into their hands 'with quiet reverence' cyclostyled copies of two brief letters 'on the thinnest of paper'. The letters ran:

>   10am, 21 April, 1967
>   YDRA
>
> My dear –
> I don't know when or whether we shall see each other again. There has been a coup d'état. Everyone is stunned. At ten minute intervals, a

new announcement of restrictions is made over the army-controlled radio. Naval school cadets sit at tables under the shuttererd post office. The mayor leans against a pillar outside the cafenon, fingering his watchchain.

It is the end of our time.

22nd of April, 1967
YDRA

My dearest
For fear of censorship, I dare not send this letter. But something has to be put down on paper.

It is a soft and fragrant night. Little owls are calling one another under the stars.

Yesterday was a day of storm, both in nature and in the life of this unhappy country. It is the time of year when yellow daisies grow thick between the whitewashed houses. Yesterday the sky hung grey, the sea raved, shipwreck was on the tongue.

Today, there are no ships; no caiquis with fruit and vegetables have come to the island. No telephone, cables, letters, or newspapers.[102]

This act of letter-giving was itself a consummate piece of theatre. The missives are both personal gift and professional prompt. Were these letters authentic documents, written by Chamberlain on the morning of the coup and the following day? Or were they dramatic creations – no less authentic for that – written expressly for this resonant moment in the wings? In Prichard-Jones Hall that night, with the tension building amid the sound of the audience settling itself into the unorthodox space beyond, each member of the cast became Chamberlain's 'dear' and 'dearest', addressee of those Greek epistles – part communiqué, part cry – that announced 'the end of our time'.

The Protagonists: 'Thinking Furiously'

The Protagonists is a piece of metatheatre, concerned throughout to reveal its own theatricality: 'Now you, in the first cage, being so careful to keep out of the limelight, why are you trying to hide from the audience?' (p. 31); 'it's not the time for melodramatic gestures' (p. 58). Chamberlain frequently employs recognisable estrangement techniques – the *Verfremdungseffekts* of Brechtian Epic theatre – through which the audience is jolted out of an imaginative surrender to the play's illusion and pushed towards an analytical evaluation of the represented human and political crisis. (Chamberlain told William Tydeman in the *Spectrum* interview that she would like the audience 'to go away thinking furiously', agreeing with him that the play encouraged a 'bifocal' attention to both existential and political matters.) Similar alienation effects are generated by the play's stylised elements: the flanking orientation of the spoken Preface and Conclusion; the use of parodic totalitarian 'edicts' (some based on actual loudspeaker and radio announcements); and the metaperspectives reminiscent of a classical tragic chorus. At the same time, the play's investment in the poetic and lyrical – most clearly present in the woman L's enunciations of maternal loss and longing, taken from Chamberlain's 1966 journal – establishes a counter-discourse (or dissident code) that challenges the cold imperatives of the official edicts and works to counteract the audience's estrangement from the action. L's history of hurt, her maternal concern, and the phobic responses ('Don't touch me. You are unclean') and lewd comments ('O, boy: two [breasts], full as gourds') to which she is subjected gesture at Chamberlain's own emotional fractures. Under constant threat from the prisoners' profanities (witness the caustic exposé of the honeyed rhetoric of tourism: 'How's this for next season's slogan? Delectable island, solid rock, no vegetation – Set in the fucking sea'), L's lyricism and that of others also *knowingly* brave the nostalgic. In having L translate the (false?) demoniac Z's gabbled sentences from the Roman Missal, Chamberlain infuses the play with further liturgical qualities that challenges the warders' (and the Junta's) predilection for univocal clarity.

The Protagonists is clearly indebted to a number of prominent post-war plays in its synthesis of Epic, existentialist and absurdist elements. Reviewing the play in *Forecast* in October 1968, Lindsay Hutchinson and Simon Sherwin rightly identified its methods as a synthesis of 'classical Greek drama, vaudeville and circus in the manner of [James] Saunders, Beckett, Ionesco, [Peter] Weiss and Sartre'.[103] Sartre's *Huis Clos* (No Exit, 1944) is an undoubted influence, particularly in its study of the metaphysical and psychological 'inscapes'[104] of incarceration. (Revising her account of her first trip to Greece in 1962 for publication, Chamberlain described the corridors of her hotel in Basle as 'endless and endless and silent. The world of Huis Clos'.)[105] Friedrich Dürrenmatt's *Die Physiker* (The Physicists) – first performed in 1962, and staged by the RSC the following year in James Kirkup's translation – is also a major exemplar and dynamic prompt. Its asylum power struggle, its plot device of feigned madness and its characteristic comic grotesqueries[106] all have parallels in *The Protagonists*. One of the most striking structural elements of *Die Physiker* – its stylised reversal of roles and ironic recycling of speeches – is adopted by Chamberlain as she alters the prison island's power dynamics in the second half of the play, making ironic 'breed-brothers' of Z (played by Jeff Thompson, a Bangor student), H (Vasilis Politis, an exile from Ídhra) and the Edict Maker (Ian Lean, a Bangor research student): 'Look at those two men, the Edict Maker and Z. I suppose you realize their roles are interchangeable?' (p. 45). (That 'interchangeability' was visually reinforced by the actors' costumes: Z wore a monk's tunic, while the Edict Maker was ironically 'dressed all in black . . . rather like a Greek Orthodox Cleric'.)[107] Such dramatic recalibrations are related to the ways in which personal identities are constituted by political documents, and erased and violently reassigned (through physical branding), throughout the play: 'It has been discovered who you are not, not who you are, which is a matter for further enquiry' (p. 32). In this regard, *The Protagonists* speaks not only to contemporary anxieties concerning dictatorship, militarism, institutionalised torture and the rise of the Far Right in a Greece currently suffering economic crisis, but also to our unease regarding our society's systems of panoptic surveillance and control. Dürrenmatt's theatre swerves from Brecht's in its resistance to the concept of an implied (or explicit) achievable 'solution' to the staged crisis;[108] Chamberlain too can be seen to adopt such a stance, which bespeaks not political quietism, but a nuanced sense of the individual's lack of control over his/her own fate. *The Protagonists* also absorbs on both local and structural levels modalities of Ionesco's and Beckett's Theatre of the Absurd and Pinter's Theatre of Menace. As for Peter Weiss's play, *Marat/Sade* (a possible influence on Chamberlain's play in its asylum setting, its alienation affects, its focus on a particular historical event and its equation of drama and violence), what Peter Brook wrote in 1965 in the introduction to the first English version holds true of *The Protagonists* itself:

> One of the London critics attacked the play on the ground[s] that it was a fashionable mixture of all the best theatrical ingredients around – Brechtian – didactic – absurdist – Theatre of Cruelty. He said this to disparage but I repeat this as praise.

> Weiss saw the use of every one of these idioms
> and he saw that he needed them all.[109]

It should be remembered that while *The Protagonists* may well seem a somewhat eccentric and outlandish (literally) work for a Bangor theatre audience in 1968, the play found a place in a culture already partly attuned to its avant-garde European identity. As already mentioned, Gwenlyn Parry's *Saer Doliau* had in 1966 energised Welsh theatre (and Eisteddfod commissions) with its subtle inflections of the Absurd. In the year in which *The Protagonists* was staged, Wilbert Lloyd Roberts's Cwmni Theatr Cymru toured with three Ionesco plays in Welsh translation.[110] The two performances of *The Protagonists* on 11 and 12 October 1968 coincided with the end of the 'National Drama Festival of Wales', sponsored – as was Chamberlain's play – by the North Wales Arts Association. Playing in Llangefni, across the Menai Bridge on Anglesey, on the same night as the final performance of *The Protagonists* was the Welsh Theatre Company's staging of Gwenlyn Parry's *Tŷ ar y Tywod* (A House on Sand). The festival had included stagings by accomplished local companies of works by Ibsen, G. M. Martens and André Obey, and Sean O'Casey.[111] The 'poetic theatre'[112] of Synge – as noted, a significant influence on 'the Greek tragic pattern' of Chamberlain's *Tide-race* – is also an ingredient in the makeup of *The Protagonists*: L's tragic 'keening', her female aloneness, and the sense of fatedness governing the play stand in a direct line of descent from Synge via *Tide-race*.[113] A specifically Welsh model for Chamberlain is of course Dylan Thomas's play for voices, *Under Milk Wood* (to which, as the Notes in the present edition reveal, there is at least one allusion in *The Protagonists*). Chamberlain's contending, often cacophonous, vocalities ask the audience to experience the work as a play for voices as well as a piece of theatre.

While the genesis of *The Protagonists* in Ídhra's overheard dialogues must not be forgotten, its theatrical genetics, as outlined above, reveal the breadth and depth of Chamberlain's familiarity with contemporary trends in European drama. Her decision to locate a play responding to the 1967 Colonels' Coup in this theatrical genealogy is itself a political intervention. As the credits roll at the end of Costa-Gavras's famous political thriller of 1969, *Z* (which focuses on the assassination of the socialist deputy Grigoris Lambrakis by far-right extremists in 1963), a list appears of those things banned by the Junta. They include the work of Ionesco, Sartre, Pinter and Beckett. (Also banned is the letter 'Z', since it was used as an opposition rallying cry: zi = 'He [Lambrakis] lives'. This fact invests the character Z in *The Protagonists* with further oppositional significance.) In its evacuation of meaning and its challenge to notions of heroic, providential destiny, the Theatre of the Absurd, as Stratos Constantinidis notes, 'deviated from the official ideology' of the Junta.[114] Constantinidis characterises the 'postmodern Greek drama' of the Junta period as a theatre of 'existential protest' that 'refused to imitate reality and thus perpetuate repressive models'. Instead, dramatists developed 'as a sign of protest, a highly personal language which was often incomprehensible to general audiences'.[115] In its evocation of irrationality, claustrophobia, imprisonment, moral and physical 'fatigue', and what Philip Hager calls 'closed-circuit' space, *The Protagonists* can be located in the company of such Greek works as Mourselas's *Dangerous Cargo* (1970), Karras's *The Escort* (1971), and Anagnostaki's *Antonio* (1972) – all of which have strong absurdist traits.[116] Thus, despite Chamberlain's protestations that *The Protagonists* was not 'political propaganda in any way' but rather 'an emotional reaction to the beastliness of the situation', her choice of absurdist framing is itself a dissident, anti-Junta act.[117] In addition, by indulging in language games, the play also contests the ideological underpinnings of a regime that was, as already noted, suspicious of metaphoricity and linguistic play. Surrealist-inspired word association, destabilising puns ('bumper size; family size; suisize', p. 56) and misprisions that quibblingly generate ironic new meanings ('O: It is easier to act a part than to live it. J: Tact won't solve anything', p. 42) are all anti-Junta weapons. Parody and the reinflection of 'traditional protest songs that had been incorporated into the national discourse' were strategies adopted by the Greek populace as modes of protest;[118] both are also deployed in *The Protagonists*. Other modes of dissent include Chamberlain's ludic references to acts of (self-)censorship ('May I quote a deleted passage from near the end of my fourth forthcoming book?'), and what one might call the politics of flowers: L's memory of past freedoms is movingly articulated through the poetry of floral lists, which ironise and render imaginatively bankrupt such (actual) slogans of the Junta as 'Greeks, pure and of a superb race, let the flowers of regeneration bloom out of the debris of the regime of falsehood'.[119]

As is evident from Alan McPherson's extant annotated acting script, the most significant changes to the written play made by the Director, David Lyn, involved paring down or excising the passages of loudspeaker edicts in English and French (these deletions are marked in the Notes to this edition). It is clear that Lyn was seeking to balance the plays' interest in the farcical theatricality, ideological emptiness and self-ironising propensities of the Greek regime's diktats with the need to keep the action fluid; the argument seems to have been not with the technique *per se* – it was a trick that could not be missed as a parodic weapon – but with the extent to which it was deployed. (Owen Garmon, who played J, valuably conceptualises the difficulty he had in adapting his performance 'to the specific demands of the staging – each character a separate entity; everyone in their own cell; no opportunity to move; everything dependent on facial expression and voice'.[120]) A certain fluidity – indeed, a volatility – was also achieved by reassigning certain solo passages to a number of speakers, which had the added effect of collapsing the distinctions between the prisoners and eroding their individuality – an outcome in tune with the wider agenda of the play.

Alan McPherson remembers the response of the audience as 'polite'; however, there were also 'one or two shouts from the Marxist elements'. For the artist and filmmaker, Clive Whalley, the play's 'political commitment' was 'easy to remember'.[121] The review of *The Protagonists* that appeared that October in the student newspaper, *Forecast*, offers the most detailed and sustained contemporary response to the play, together with an insight into the factional political landscape of Bangor's student body in 1968. The authors were Lindsay Hutchinson – at that time an ex-student of English who ran a Maoist bookshop ('Bookbane') in Upper Bangor – and Simon Sherwin – a student drama director/producer who had by 1968 staged, to acclaim, productions of Brecht's *The Tutor* and Weiss's *Marat/Sade*.[122] Unabashedly Maoist, their tendentious review praises the 'aplomb' with which the cast and crew realised their project. But they characterised the audience's applause as 'of that nervous kind which follows contact with Debussy's lyricism, or more pertinently, Beethoven's madness'.[123] *The Protagonists* was a discredited bourgeois affair, 'rich . . . in poetic and dramatic inventiveness', certainly, but 'ideologically bankrupt' in its 'sustained hysteria' and self-indulgent aestheticism ('*The Protagonists* seems to stand in the same relation to Greece, to quote Marx, "as onanism to sexual love"'). For the reviewers, the play's claim to 'solidarity with the people of Greece' was fatally undermined by Chamberlain's refusal 'to see the facts in political terms'. An 'incoherence' bred of bourgeois false consciousness; insoluble ambiguities; overdetermined symbolism ('We are drenched with water symbols which can be construed as either the Greek islands, the sea around them, or the forces that fertilise them'); and the obfuscations of allegory all render illusory the possibility of meaningful political intervention. What such a critique clearly misses is the way in which the play itself articulates precisely these anxieties regarding the euphemisms of writerly protest and the deferrals of artistic representation; as A remarks: 'I know how you'd end it, coward. Say it was a dream, go so far as to say it's allegorical, that dirty word! Say it was a myth' (pp. 55–6). The claim that Chamberlain was suggesting that 'all we can do is preserve our right to lonely lyricism' disregards the ways in which the play's poetic invocations of an idealised past are self-consciously called into question by the grand and petty violences of the present, and by the rapaciousness – 'Shit and fuck!' – of the play's invasive discourses.

Post-*Protagonists*: Chamberlain's Agon

The play has never been performed since. This is partly due, of course, to the fact that it was not published. Chamberlain's metropolitan publisher, Hodder and Stoughton, 'helped with the typing', but a publishing house that specialised in fiction and non-fiction was not a viable outlet for such a work.[124] There was some hope of following up the two Bangor performances with stagings in Coventry, Cambridge and London, but nothing came of this.[125] Chamberlain's post-*Protagonists* world was becoming increasingly lonely and fraught. Financial worries certainly contributed to her anxieties. Alan McPherson describes her move in November

1968 from the familiar territory of Upper Bangor to a flat in Chateau (now Plas) Rhianfa on Anglesey – 'some insanely rich person's dream of a French Chateau', which 'had the air of a seedy but once opulent hotel' – as a 'disaster'. McPherson imagines an exiled Chamberlain looking out 'across the Menai Straits at the Island of Upper Bangor'. The 'refugee' Chamberlain had 'run out of rooms to borrow for a few weeks or months' in Bangor, and so had to negotiate a 'transition across the strait and narrow', as McPherson punningly recalls.[126] He attended a flat-warming party at Chateau Rhianfa that uncannily mirrored the farewell party that had been thrown for Chamberlain in April of the same year, before she returned to Ídhra and the coup. McPherson emphasises that the move was an 'intense event' for her:

> All her friends here together in Rhianfa for one glorious evening, then everybody gone home: 'Goodnight, Brenda, goodnight' . . . She could not work. She was on her own. It was the wrong island. On the Island of Upper Bangor her pattern of work had revolved around her social life of calling in on people, a coffee here, a cup of tea there, a chat on the street, carrying gossip from one side of the island to the other. Then she would disappear into her workplace and work furiously for a few hours and then be out again, skipping from one place to another . . . The two removals, from people and from work, bound her into a depressed state.

Fascinatingly, one detects in McPherson's recollection of Chamberlain 'carrying gossip from one side of the island to the other' an unconscious, disquieting echo of the opening of *The Protagonists*: 'This creature had brought a secret message from another island, carrying poison between its narrow teeth'. More than forty years on, McPherson maps the Lérian world of *The Protagonists* onto the islands of Upper Bangor and the exilic Isle of Anglesey.

Since her return to Bangor in December 1967, Chamberlain had been seeking to complete two projects intimately related to *The Protagonists*. The first was a Beckettian 'play', begun on Ídhra, that is identified in the fourth of its five surviving versions as a script for a film 'to be shot in the open air on winter location, North Wales coast, Irish sea'.[127] The setting is a 'derelict copper mine in the middle of a fertile island'; a 'blood-coloured lake fills the westward end of the mine-bottom'. Crouched in a battered car 'on the lip-edge of the chasm' are four men (Antoniadis, Paion, Bistas – the 'one-legged man' of the title – and Stamnos); in the surrounding 'landscape' are a nun; a woman – Siassanis Philotis – whom the men identify as a prostitute, thus making her a version of L in *The Protagonists*; the king; and 'an army battalion', whose troops wear 'masks of horned sheep-skulls'.[128] The fourth version resurrects into dramatic life 'The Black Bride' from Chamberlain's 1965 graphic work on Ídhra, discussed above. A single Beckettian thorn tree, from which the two women are described as 'indistinguishable', renders the terrain starkly symbolic. Inchoate though the work is, it is identifiably an absurdist figuring of certain events that followed the Colonels' Coup (most clearly the king's attempted 'counter-revolution'). The work shows Chamberlain exploring the ways in which the Greek crisis – and again, the dislocations of her own post-coup condition – might be articulated through a Beckettian dramatic mode, a pared-down *mise-en-scène*, and cinematographic techniques.

The second work – far more substantial, though also unfinished – is entitled *The Monument*. The title is the nickname of the central character, T (also known as the 'Tall Man') – clearly modelled on the composer and left-wing deputy Mikis Theodorakis, whose music was banned by the Junta under Army Decree No. 13. Theodorakis (who was to write the score to Costa-Gavras's film, *Z*) was arrested in August 1967 and jailed; in January 1968, he was exiled with his family to Zatouna, a mountain village in western Arcadia, on the Peloponnese peninsula. In *The Monument*, Chamberlain's tubercular T is a 'composer of popular music' who has been banished to a remote village – identified specifically as Zatouna – 'high in the mountains of Arkadia . . . a natural prison, surrounded on three sides by mountain peaks and torrent beds'.[129] He is 'a symbol above and beyond politics, of resistance to the military rule'. Thus Theodorakis's internal exile in January 1968 gives us a *terminus post quem* for Chamberlain's play, which establishes it as a 'Welsh' work, post-dating her return to Bangor. Again, Chamberlain deploys drama to expose the physical and psychological consequences of the Junta's anathemas; at the same time, she was gaining objective purchase on a personal predicament – the loss of creative energy. Watched over by two guards – a monolithic 'triple object' into which he feels his identity has been swallowed – T remarks:

> I have lost the desire to create. The singer in my head has died or gone away, or been beaten to death.
>
> . . .
>
> Round and round[,] the trap, the walls; no fresh tunes run in my head; stale words wander there, words printed on a black tumour, where before white walls and sunbursts shone.[130]

T's 'beautiful and neurotic' wife, Nana ('a suffragette at the stage of European women at the beginning of this century, fighting so late for emancipation, Greek style') seeks to shore up what remains of T's dissident identity, characterising her husband's political exile in absurdist terms as a grotesque 'game', 'same as everything else in life. You must invent the rules of play, your way and not theirs. Look at the insane; how they get away with anything'.[131] *The Monument* and *The Protagonists* are co-texts that explore incarceration in political, psychological and metaphysical incarnations, and which ponder the quandary raised directly by T: 'when the pattern of life breaks, what positive act can get us out of the gin, heaven knows . . . so few can spring the trap'. 'In Athens', T remarks, 'time leapt like a happy cat. Here, it is a dying animal'.[132] The echo is of 'Sailing to Byzantium' ('Consume my heart away; sick with desire / And fastened to a dying animal / It knows not what it is') – W. B. Yeats's ambivalent, self-ironising meditation on the appeal of the self-sufficient world of art and of 'Monuments of unageing intellect'. Like Yeats's poem, Chamberlain's *The Monument* exposes the *deathliness* of the 'monumental' (whether artistic reputation or stone memorial), as against the needs and desires of 'tremulous flesh'. And like *The Protagonists*, *The Monument* remains self-consciously sceptical regarding wistful longing: 'Nostalgia', says T, 'is the great agony'.[133] Towards the end of the final typescript version of the play, Chamberlain quotes in translation the concluding lines of one of Giorgos Seferis's most celebrated poems:

> The ships hoot now that dusk falls on Piraeus,
> hoot and hoot, but no capstan moves,
> no chain gleams wet in the vanishing light,
> the captain stands like a stone in white & gold.

> Wherever I travel Greece wounds me,
> curtains of mountains, archipelagos, naked granite.
> They call the one ship that sails AG ONIA 937.

> > m/s [motor ship] *Aulis*, waiting to sail.
> > Summer 1936[134]

Looking out from Chateau Rhianfa at the dark start of 1969, Chamberlain was also confronted with 'curtains of mountains, archipelagos, naked granite' and was facing her own 'agony'.

She checked herself into North Wales Hospital in Denbigh for psychiatric treatment. Her evisceratingly candid response to her time there – astonishingly, marked for potential publication in the journal *Mabon* – is reminiscent of some of the more anguished sections of her 1966 journal, but surpasses that document both in its articulation of dread – 'I don't want to be turned into a cabbage'; E[lectric]S[chock]T[reatment] morning, Apprehension[,] not to say stark fear' – and in its cold assessment of the treatment and therapy she was receiving: 'The smoke-filled brain is X-rayed, shocked by electric impulses[;] whims and dreams are analysed'.[135] Though painfully aware of the gulf (in all senses) between herself and the political internees of Greece, Denbigh must have felt like her Welsh Léros – that island of sanatoria and prison camps. The Greece she does evoke in the hospital journal is that of pre-coup Ídhra, which, balm-like, floods the pathologies of the present:

> This is where I hit myself in the back of the head.
> This is the bin, the tunnel of echoes, the sick place.
> The corridors are filled with distorted faces, faces without magnetism, bodies without fire.
>
> Beauty is proscribed.
>
> In Greece at this moment the island boys are throwing themselves into the foaming sea, knowing exactly where they are, and where they are going.
>
> Here, nobody has a purpose. Slow tears, like those of the birth-giving turtle, run on many faces.[136]

Agonisingly, in its move from visceral self-analysis to a statement that could equally be an edict ('Beauty is proscribed') and then to a lyrical conjuring of the past, the passage might have come from *The Protagonists*. The Denbigh journal comports itself stylistically and generically to the play that, in its hybrid dramatic and confessional elements, is the culmination of all Chamberlain's experiences and experiments. In a brief late essay entitled 'The Relationship Between Art and Literature', she even claimed that the tension she had always felt between her art and her writing had been resolved – had 'most perfectly come together' – in *The Protagonists*.[137] Sitting in her hospital bed in Denbigh, 'looking towards the ruined castle', she turns to Greece; heartbreakingly, the accents are those of her own dramatic creation, L.

A move back to Upper Bangor (first to Glanrafon Hill, then back to Menai View Terrace) after she had discharged herself from Denbigh meant that she found herself once more among a small network of friends. That coterie celebrated the appearance in 1969 of her *Poems with Drawings*, which features excerpts from *The Protagonists* (now configured visually as poetry) in counterpoint with her 'islographs' of Greek rock-shapes. These poems and artworks became a Welsh Arts Council touring exhibition the following year, which also saw the publication of *Alun Lewis and the Making of the Caseg Broadsheets*. But the depression that haunted her, Fury-like, could not be kept at bay. As Holman notes, in May 1971 she exhibited 'a series of fragile, psychologically telling sketches of a young woman; bound or weighted, or rooted to the ground'.[138] A barbiturate overdose on 8 July 1971 was a cry for help that came too late; she died three days later and was buried in Glanadda Cemetery, Bangor. Alan McPherson cannot remember attending a funeral where so few people were present. Chamberlain's epitaph – 'I was born to live / I was born to die' – echoes the bleak yet brave teleology articulated by J at the end of the stark sequence of prisoner micro-biographies in *The Protagonists*:

J: I was born
to have
to be
to drink
to sleep.
A: I was born
to see
to hear
to speak
to read.
L: I was born
to do
to arrive
to remain
to depart.
O: I was born
to begin
to know
to give
to take.
J: I was born
to learn
to be able to die.
(p. 14)

[1] Brenda Chamberlain, *The Green Heart* (London: Oxford University Press, 1958), p. 35. For a discussion of Chamberlain's life and work under the rubric of 'islandness', see Damian Walford Davies, *Cartographies of Culture: New Geographies of Welsh Writing in English* (Cardiff: University of Wales Press, 2012), pp. 78–171.

[2] See Katherine Elizabeth Holman, 'The Literary Achievement of Brenda Chamberlain' (unpublished MA thesis, University College of Swansea, 1976), p. 229.

[3] See Conran's 'Praise Song for Eirlys', in *Castles: Variations on an Original Theme* (Llandysul: Gomer, 1993), p. 85.

[4] Brenda Chamberlain, autobiographical essay in Meic Stephens (ed.), *Artists in Wales* (Llandysul: Gomer, 1971), p. 52.

[5] Brenda Chamberlain, *A Rope of Vines: Journal from a Greek Island* (London: Hodder and Stoughton, 1965), p. 14. Hereafter *RoV*.

[6] Quoted in Holman, 'The Literary Achievement of Brenda Chamberlain', pp. 35 and 91.

[7] See H. J. Fleure, 'The Welsh People', *Wales*, 10 (October 1939), pp. 265, 266, 268.

[8] Linda Adams, '"Fieldwork": The Caseg Broadsheets and the Welsh Anthropologist', *Welsh Writing in English: A Yearbook of Critical Essays*, 5 (1999), p. 55.

[9] Robin Skelton, *The Writings of J. M. Synge* (London: Thames and Hudson, 1997), p. 48.

[10] Brenda Chamberlain, *Tide-race* (London: Hodder and Stoughton, 1962), p. 222.

[11] Brenda Chamberlain, 'Abstract of a Journey 1962', *Mabon*, 1, 3 (Summer 1970), pp. 16–26.

[12] National Library of Wales, MS 21499E, p. 6.

[13] Ibid., p. 12.

[14] Ibid., p. 17.

[15] Ibid., p. 20.

[16] Ibid., p. 24.

[17] Ibid., p. 22.

[18] Ibid., p. 25.

[19] Ibid.

[20] Ibid.

[21] Ibid.

[22] Kate Holman, *Brenda Chamberlain* (Cardiff: University of Wales Press, 1997), p. 9.

[23] Anthony Conran, 'The Writings of Brenda Chamberlain', *The Anglo-Welsh Review*, 20, 46 (Spring 1972), p. 21.

[24] Lawrence Durrell, *Prospero's Cell: A Guide to the Landscape and Manners of the Island of Corcyra* (1945; London: Faber and Faber, 2000), p. 1.

[25] See David H. Close, *Greece Since 1945: Politics, Economy and Society* (London: Longman, 2002), pp. 104–7.

[26] For Chamberlain's drawings of Saragas, see her journal of 1964, National Library of Wales, MS 21518C. See also Maurice Cooke, 'The Painting of Brenda Chamberlain', *Anglo-Welsh Review*, 20, 46 (Spring, 1972), pp. 14–15: '[Chamberlain] thus describes the evolution of her style in this connection: "The first tentative drawings were naturalistic . . . then they became stylised. The naturalistic line was about to break. A sort of alphabet of the dance began to evolve from letting my hand move without inhibition, leaving the contours of the body to look after themselves. I began to feel that these signs were moving, that perhaps someone looking at them could with a little practice see what position the dancer had moved from, and to what position he was approaching. In other words I was beginning to identify myself with the choreography"'. For Chamberlain's collaboration with 'an Egyptian composer of electronic music', Halim El Dabh (1921–, Professor Emeritus of African Ethnomusicology at Kent State University, Ohio), see Chamberlain's letter of 7 March 1965 to Alan Clodd (National Library of Wales, MS 23881D/31–2): 'He played several of his own compositions to me – I sat near with a pen and notebook.

In response to the notes, a kind of shorthand came on the paper. When the composer came to look at them afterwards, he found that he could play back from my drawings, could read the marks as though they were traditional notation. We both felt that new ground had been broken. I had all summer been drawing movement, so perhaps I had unknowingly been preparing myself for these strange abstract signs'.

[27] Close, *Greece Since 1945*, p. 108.

[28] Cooke, 'The Painting of Brenda Chamberlain', p. 11.

[29] See ibid., pp. 11–12.

[30] See the discussion of Chamberlain's 'Blodeuwedd' (which appeared in *Wales* in 1946), in Walford Davies, *Cartographies of Culture*, pp. 107–9.

[31] Cooke, 'The Painting of Brenda Chamberlain', p. 11.

[32] 'A Total Eclipse of the Sun', *Mabon*, 1, 5 (Spring 1972), pp. 6–13.

[33] National Library of Wales, MS 21500E, p. 28.

[34] Ibid., p. 29.

[35] Ibid., p 53.

[36] Ibid., pp. 30, 32, 30, 34, 42, 55.

[37] Ibid., p. 44.

[38] Ibid., pp. 50–1.

[39] Ibid., p. 43.

[40] Ibid., pp. 51, 35, 40.

[41] Ibid., p. 37.

[42] Ibid., pp. 36, 39.

[43] Ibid., pp. 40, 41.

[44] Ibid., p. 43.

[45] Ibid., pp. 44, 53.

[46] See ibid., pp. 34, 47.

[47] Ibid., p. 45.

[48] For Berthold Paněk, see *Tide-race*, pp. 203–10, together with the fascinating narrative of Harold Taylor ('Merfyn Edwards' in *Tide-race*), one of the lighthouse keepers on Bardsey in those dark days: 'The Light on Top', *World Lighthouse Society Newsletter*, 8,

3 (2010), pp. 8–13 (*http://www.worldlighthouses.org/WLS%20 Newsletter%203rd%20Qtr%202010.pdf*, accessed 29 July 2012).

[49] National Library of Wales, MS 21500E, p. 52.

[50] Ibid., p. 58.

[51] Close, *Greece Since 1945*, p. 108.

[52] Ibid., p. 109.

[53] Alan McPherson, 'Upper Bangor is an Island', p. 1. I am very grateful for sight of this unpublished memoir.

[54] Thomas W. Gallant, *Modern Greece* (London: Arnold, 2001), p. 198.

[55] Close, *Greece Since 1945*, p. 110.

[56] Thanos Veremis, *The Military in Greek Politics: From Independence to Democracy* (London: Hurst and Company, 1997), p. 158.

[57] C. M. Woodhouse, *Modern Greece: A Short History* (London: Faber and Faber, 1977), p. 298.

[58] See Konstantina Maragkou, 'The Wilson Government's Responses to "The Rape of Greek Democracy"', *Journal of Contemporary History*, 45, 162 (2010), pp. 162–80.

[59] Close, *Greece Since 1945*, p. 116.

[60] Richard Clogg, 'The Ideology of the "Revolution of 21 April 1967"', in Richard Clogg and George Yannopoulos (eds), *Greece Under Military Rule* (London: Secker & Warburg, 1972), pp. 37, 40.

[61] Close, *Greece Since 1945*, p. 116.

[62] See Gallant, *Modern Greece*, p. 198 and C. M. Woodhouse, 'The "Revolution" in its Historical Context', in Clogg and Yannopoulos (eds), *Greece Under Military Rule*, p. 1.

[63] Clogg, 'The Ideology of the "Revolution of 21 April 1967"', p. 40.

[64] Ibid., pp. 36, 43, 45, 51.

[65] Karen van Dyck, *Cassandra and the Censors: Greek Poetry Since 1967* (Ithaca and London: Cornell University Press, 1998), p. 16.

[66] Rodis Roufos, 'Culture and the Military', in Clogg and Yannopoulos (eds), *Greece Under Military Rule*, pp. 150, 156.

[67] van Dyck, *Cassandra and the Censors*, p. 19.

[68] See ibid., pp. 19–20.

[69] 'Well, I'll just say there were lovely flowers there', *Forecast*, May 1968, p. 18. See Appendix 3, p. 117 below.

[70] National Library of Wales Sound Archive: Reel-to-reel tape (RM 16699) and CD (6772).

[71] Autobiographical essay in Meic Stephens (ed.), *Artists in Wales*, p. 52.

[72] As Marc Dubin reminds us, Léros still suffers from a 'domestic image problem' that is 'compounded by its name, the butt of jokes by off-islanders, who pounce on its similarity to the word *lerá* [literally, 'grime'], connoting rascality and unsavouriness'; *The Rough Guide to the Dodecanese and East Aegean Islands*, 4th edn (London: Rough Guides, 2005), pp. 289–90.

[73] *The Times*, 18 September 1967, p. 4.

[74] Ibid., 11 September 1968, p. 6.

[75] Ibid., 11 April 1968, p. 8.

[76] Ibid., 9 April 1968, p. 11 and 3 January 1970, p. 4.

[77] 'Well, I'll just say there were lovely flowers there', pp. 18–19. See Appendix 3, pp. 118–119 below.

[78] See p. 4 below for another such sketch.

[79] 'Well, I'll just say there were lovely flowers there', p. 19. See Appendix 3, p. 120 below.

[80] Ibid.

[81] Autobiographical essay in Meic Stephens (ed.), *Artists in Wales*, p. 54.

[82] Chamberlain claimed in the autobiographical essay published in 1971 in *Artists in Wales* that she 'stuck it out for twelve months' after the April 1967 coup, but her recollection was not accurate. As the interview in *Forecast* proves (see below, p. 121), she was certainly on Ídhra on 14 December 1967 when king Constantine fled to Rome following his abortive counter-coup.

[83] McPherson, 'Upper Bangor is an Island', p. 1.

[84] See Conran, *Castles: Variations on an Original Theme*, p. 85.

[85] McPherson, 'Upper Bangor is an Island', p. 1.

[86] As McPherson states, the Daniel family had experienced a cultural exile following Cathrin Daniel's conversion to Catholicism. J. E. Daniel resigned his professorship at the Bala-Bangor Congregationalist Seminary and took a new career as Inspector of Schools, first in Glamorgan and then in Flintshire. The family moved back to Bangor following his death in a car accident in 1962. Cathrin Daniel and her daughter Anna are referenced in Conran's 'Praise Song for Eirlys': see *Castles: Variations on an Original Theme*, p. 85.

[87] Holman, 'The Literary Achievement of Brenda Chamberlain', p. 210.

[88] Holman, *Brenda Chamberlain*, p. 64.

[89] 'Greek Actress Hides her Identity', *North Wales Chronicle*, 19 September 1968, p. 1.

[90] See note 70 above.

[91] [Alan Twelves], 'Theatre Plan to Boost Welsh Drama', *North Wales Chronicle*, 26 September 1968, p. 7; see Appendix 1, p. 112 below.

[92] Ibid.

[93] Ibid.

[94] The first draft of the play contained a few lines of Welsh, and in the fourth version, Chamberlain was considering using Welsh as one of the languages in which the edicts were delivered. See Notes, pp. 100 and 109 below.

[95] Alan Twelves, 'The Brenda Chamberlain Exhibition', *North Wales Chronicle*, 1 August 1968, p. 3.

[96] Holman, 'The Literary Achievement of Brenda Chamberlain', p. 211.

[97] Photocopy sent to me by Alan McPherson.

[98] See Notes, pp. 75–7 below.

[99] Joy Ostle, personal communication (19 September, 2012).

Joy (Roberts, at that time) was the stage manager, and recalls 'collecting a dead rabbit from the butcher's shop in Upper Bangor' for the two performances of the play.

[100] 'Well, I'll just say there were lovely flowers there', p. 19. See Appendix 3, p. 124 below.

[101] I am grateful to Joy Ostle for this information (personal communication, 14 September 2012).

[102] Again, I am indebted to Joy Ostle for copies of these letters, and for her account of this delicate moment (personal communication, 7, 19 and 24 September 2012).

[103] Lindsay Hutchinson and Simon Sherwin, review of *The Protagonists*, *Forecast* (University College of North Wales, Bangor student newspaper), October 1968, p. 12. See Appendix 4, p. 125 below.

[104] See Martin Esslin, *The Theatre of the Absurd*, 3rd edn (London: Methuen, 2001), p. 432.

[105] Chamberlain, 'Abstract of a Journey 1962', p. 17. Chamberlain's original journal entry describes the hotel thus: 'It could be like this in limbo'; National Library of Wales, MS 21499E, p. 3.

[106] See Urs Jenny, *Dürrenmatt: A Study of the Plays* (London: Eyre Methuen, 1978), p. 19 and Timo Tiusanen, *Dürrenmatt* (Princeton, NJ: Princeton University Press, 1977), p. 274.

[107] Joy Ostle, personal communication (24 September 2012). Ostle emphasises that the Edict Maker was 'certainly not any obvious symbol of the Greek Church'; rather, his garb suggested 'the idiocy of so much authority'.

[108] See Kenneth S. Whitton, *The Theatre of Friedrich Dürrenmatt: A Study in the Possibility of Freedom* (London: Oswald Wolff, 1980), p. 125.

[109] Peter Weiss, *Marat/Sade: The Persecution and Assassination of Marat as Performed by the Inmates of the Asylum of Charenton under the Direction of the Marquis de Sade*, trans. Geoffrey Skelton (London: Marion Boyars, 1965), p. 6.

[110] The plays were *Victimes de Devoir* (Victims of Duty, 1953), translated by Gareth Miles as *Merthyron Dyletswydd; Le Nouveau Locataire* (The New Tenant, 1955), translated as *Y Tenant Newydd* by Ken Lloyd-Jones; and *Scène à Quatre* (Foursome, 1959), translated as *Pedwarawd* by John Watkin. See Lyn T. Jones, 'Datblygiad Theatr Genedlaethol i Gymru, 1964–82', in Hazel Walford Davies (ed.), *Y Theatr Genedlaethol yng Nghymru* (Caerdydd: Gwasg Prifysgol Cymru, 2007), p. 180.

[111] See *North Wales Chronicle*, 17 October 1968, p. 9.

[112] Skelton, *The Writings of J. M. Synge*, p. 52.

[113] See Holman, 'The Literary Achievement of Brenda Chamberlain', pp. 92, 101, 109.

[114] See Stratos E. Constantinidis, 'Existential Protest in Greek Drama During the Junta', *Journal of Modern Greek Studies*, 3, 2 (October 1982), p. 138.

[115] Ibid.

[116] See ibid., p. 141 and Philip Hager, '*Antonio or the Message*: Bourgeois Conformism and the Dictatorship of the Colonels in Greece (1967–74)', *Platform*, 2, 1 ('Theatres of Resistance', Spring 2007), pp. 58, 60, 64.

[117] 'Well, I'll just say there were lovely flowers there', p. 19. See Appendix 3, p. 123 below.

[118] Gallant, *Modern Greece*, p. 202.

[119] Ibid., p. 198.

[120] Owen Garmon, personal communication (6 May 2011).

[121] I am grateful to Alan McPherson for sending me Whalley's assessment (18 June 2011).

[122] I am grateful to Alan McPherson for this information (19 July 2012).

[123] Hutchinson and Sherwin, review of *The Protagonists*, p. 12. See Appendix 4, pp. 126, 128 below.

[124] Holman, *Brenda Chamberlain*, p. 64.

[125] Alan McPherson's diary confirms the following: that meetings to discuss *The Protagonists*, together with rehearsals,

continued into January 1969; that Chamberlain was corresponding with contacts in Cambridge in December 1968; and that David Lyn and Owen Garmon travelled to Cambridge on 4 January 1969, presumably to discuss a possible performance there. I am grateful to Alan McPherson for this information (18 June 2011). See also Twelves, 'The Brenda Chamberlain Exhibition', p. 3 and Holman, *Brenda Chamberlain*, p. 10.

[126] McPherson, 'Upper Bangor is an Island', p. 3.

[127] National Library of Wales MSS 21495C, 21496E, 21497E. The work is identified as a filmscript in the fourth draft, contained in MS 21497E. See Holman, 'The Literary Achievement of Brenda Chamberlain', p. 363: 'The quantity of unfinished and abortive work which Brenda Chamberlain left on her death confirms the suggestion that she was casting about for writing inspiration, with little success. Schemes continued to occur to her. For instance in 1968 on her return to Bangor she wrote to Meic Stephens about her ambition to write a book about her own experience of the sea. She made a comparison with Rachel Carson's *The Sea Around Us* which Antoine was described as reading in *The Water-castle*'.

[128] See National Library of Wales, MS 21497E, pp. 1–5.

[129] National Library of Wales MS 21498E, p. 5.

[130] Ibid., p. 26.

[131] Ibid.

[132] Ibid., p. 57.

[133] Ibid., p. 82.

[134] Ibid., p. 101.

[135] National Library of Wales, MS 21501E, pp. 21, 32, 29.

[136] Ibid., p. 27.

[137] Ibid., p. 58. See also Jonah Jones, 'Island Artist: An Exhibition of the Work of Brenda Chamberlain', *New Welsh Review*, 1, 2 (Autumn 1988), p. 54: 'Had [Chamberlain's] late

development into multi-media expression found a greater audience, Brenda might have been still with us. Nowadays, performance art, TV, theatre and dance would all have embraced her wide-ranging creations with ease'.

[138] Holman, *Brenda Chamberlain*, p. 11.

Figure 12: National Library of Wales, ex 2735: cover of the annotated acting script belonging to Alan ('Phredd') McPherson. By kind permission of Alan McPherson.

A Note on the Text

In preparing the present edition of *The Protagonists*, I have consulted the six substantive drafts in which the play exists, as follows (the initial, abbreviated designations are my own):

Prot 1: National Library of Wales, MS 21491D – typescript first draft with autograph additions and amendments, and drawings that visualise the actors' positions on stage at various junctures.

• *Prot* 2: National Library of Wales, MS 21492D – typescript second draft with autograph amendments and drawings that visualise the actors' positions on stage.

• *Prot* 3: National Library of Wales, MS 21493D – typescript third draft with autograph amendments and drawings that visualise the actors' positions on stage.

• *Prot* 4: National Library of Wales, MS 21494E – cyclostyled 'acting script' with autograph amendments; effectively fourth draft.

• *Prot* 5: Gwynedd Archives and Museums Service, Caernarfon Record Office; North Wales Arts Association Archive, XD90/3/11 Brenda Chamberlain – typescript acting script, later than *Prot* 4.

• *Prot* 6: National Library of Wales, ex 2735 – annotated acting script belonging to Alan ('Phredd') McPherson, who played the Guard (typescript with supplementary handwritten pages). Identical to *Prot* 5, except in the following respects:

a) in *Prot* 6, the Preface (which lacks the first two

lines of its counterpart in *Prot* 5) and Conclusion are handwritten on exercise-book leaves and interleaved; b) while pp. 3–4 of *Prot* 5 are taken up with preliminary stage directions, pp. 3–4 of *Prot* 6 (hand numbered, on smaller leaves) contain the character assessments of 'The Black Dossier' (see Notes, pp. 75–6); c) in *Prot* 6, the final sheet (pp. 71 and 72, backed) is torn in half.

It is reasonable to assume that *Prot* 6 is an annotated 'performance' copy of the 'core' text, *Prot* 5.

Prot 1 was written on Ídhra. Chamberlain worked on *Prot* 2–*Prot* 5 in Bangor after her return from Greece in December 1967.

For this edition, *Prot* 5 is taken as base text. Punctuation in *Prot* 5 is erratic; given the requirements of a published text, I have punctuated in order to achieve clarity of syntax and sense where necessary. (Of course, *The Protagonists* is a play that sets out to perplex syntax and sense as a dramatic effect; these deliberate confusions have naturally been preserved.) In places, I have also judged that altering lineation aids intelligibility. Nowhere have the dramatic/vocal effects created by Chamberlain's original layout been sacrificed. Processes of clarification have been aided by collation of the text's other drafts and Chamberlain's manuscripts in the National Library of Wales. Various textual cruxes and editorial decisions are outlined in the notes.

Alan McPherson's annotated acting copy (*Prot* 6) is an invaluable resource in that it offers a privileged insight into the way in which *The Protagonists* was actually staged. The Notes record the substantive ways in which the play, as performed, differed from the base text of *Prot* 5.

The Protagonists

The Protagonists was first performed by the Welsh Drama Studio in the Prichard-Jones Hall (apsidal end), University College of North Wales, Bangor, at 8pm on 11 and 12 October 1968, with the following cast:

Guard	Alan ('Phredd') McPherson
Edict Maker	Ian Lean
A	Gwyn Parry
L	Sophia Michopoulou
J	Owen Garmon
O	Gray Evans
Z	Jeff Thompson
H	Vasilis Politis

Producer	David Lyn
Assistant to the Producer and Stage Manager	Joy Roberts
Assistant Stage Manager	Joan Rees
Sound & Special Effects	Brian Ogden
Lighting created by	Dr C. P. Spencer
Costumes designed by	Edith Stanley
Wardrobe Mistress	Janice Housley
Business Managers	Eirlys McPherson and Anna Daniel
Photography by	Emyr Roberts

The performance programme recorded the following 'Production Acknowledgements': 'Scaffolding for the set was loaned from U.C.N.W. Maintenance Department. The hall was hired from U.C.N.W. Bangor'. The price of admission was 7/6.

THE PROTAGONISTS

PRO   PRO   PRO

TAGON   TAGON

AGONISTS   THE AGONISTS

Brenda Chamberlain
Ydra 1967
October – November

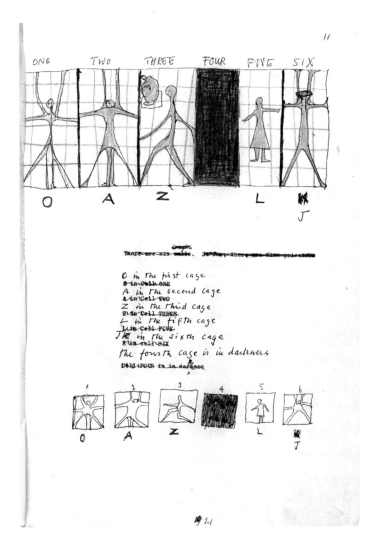

Figure 13: National Library of Wales MS 21493D, p. 11: Brenda Chamberlain's drawing of the prisoners' attitudes at the beginning of *The Protagonists*, from the third version of the play. Llyfrgell Genedlaethol Cymru/The National Library of Wales.

Preface

As the woman L shall say in an hour or so,

'Don't let it shock you.'

Give me a dry bone, and I'll turn it to nourishment:

A garden here, roast quail there, twin water-fountains in the near distance.

For winter, a Turkish room; for summer, a grove of wind-catcher pine trees; for spring, love; for autumn, melancholy; winter a looking forward to a better time.

Who wants a *better* time?

Why can't now be good?

Before the action commences, the stage is empty for some time, but there is a lot of noise from the wings: clashing of iron gates, keys falling, shouts, running feet, angry protests. This continues while members of the audience are taking their seats.

Young men in tracksuits carry the six cages onto the stage in sections and assemble them, after which they furnish them with truckle-beds and stools.

The cages are placed at a slight distance from one another. The stool in cage 3 is high, such as is used for lions to crouch on.

A sound off: locks being opened, gates clashing to, shouts, the crack of a long whip. Loud bootsteps of six men.

Enter GUARD *with lion whip, thrusting five prisoners before him. He threatens them into their cages: O into cage 1, A into cage 2, Z (with whom he has trouble, Z snarling and throwing his head from side to side like a lion with a heavy mane) into cage 3, L into cage 5, J into cage 6.*

The GUARD *is dressed after the fashion of a circus lion trainer crossed with a ringmaster: oiled black hair; long moustache; frogged tail-coat (scarlet with white frogging and gilt buttons); too-widely-cut riding breeches; and black riding boots. He is heavy-torsoed, very slender-legged. A holster and pistol disturb the balance of his coat on the right side. As tamer, he is careful not to turn his back on the prisoners until they are locked into their cages.*

Cage 4 is empty so far, and in darkness.

The prisoners take up their positions in the cages, each in the centre of his square except for Z who is pacing from wall to wall.

L feels the air around her. The men stand with their legs wide apart and arms in a horizontal position. They slowly raise their arms above their heads as they draw their feet together, then return to their original positions.

They are measuring the width of their new world under the controlling whip of the GUARD.

Each cage is lit by a naked lightbulb in the centre of the ceiling, except for untenanted cage 4.

L looks Egyptian, neither young nor old, intensely nervous, histrionic, with large ugly hands that she twists together passionately. She moves without grace in large bounds, which men find attractive for its suggestion of painful freedom. Her hair is straight and black and disregarded. Her skin very white, eyes almond-shaped, nose hawklike. Sensuous mouth.

Z, unlike the other prisoners, is in white clothing from head to foot: a monk's cowl, heavy cotton tunic belted with a thick cord, worn low on the hips in the old Russian style, woollen trousers, heavy boots laced to the knees. He has long matted hair, a ragged beard. The rest are in prison dress. L's frock is of a lighter grey than the trousers and jackets of the men.

The GUARD *paces the stage slowly, inspecting the 'animals' in their cages.*

With a final long, trailing crack of the whip, beginning along the fronts of the cages and ending along the floor of the stage, he is satisfied that all is in order and so leaves –

> O *in the first cage*
> A *in the second cage*
> Z *in the third cage*
> L *in the fifth cage*
> J *in the sixth cage*
> *The fourth cage is in darkness.*

Having measured to their satisfaction, the prisoners come forward to the bars and begin to speak.

IT BEGINS

A: The men who are in power have expelled us to a certain rock of so hopeless a ship's passage it discourages all but the most determined or insensitive voyagers. The rats followed on a rodent ship. We have become breed-brothers, indistinguishable. Hardship has brought out the hairy likenesses.

O: It is time for the worst to happen.

L: The stars have not been prophetic.

A: Rats everywhere. A swollen corpse on a step at the post office, bedded in torn-up letters.

O: The ones for whom we wait never come.

A: This creature had brought a secret message from another island, carrying poison between its narrow teeth.

L: But it didn't get far.

O: How could it, with spies everywhere?

A: So they killed it – no names – the postmaster, or the bald informer, or a girl-child who knew the art of the perfectly-aimed fist or foot.

(*The* EDICT MAKER *comes in, followed by the* GUARD. *At sight of the two officials, the prisoners back discreetly to their stools. Z is still pacing up and down. The* EDICT MAKER *is a slight, youngish military type, unexcitable, without distinguishing features. Dressed in a field-grey uniform with a peaked cap, he gives an impression of efficiency. His only expression is a tight smile.*)

O: It stinks.

A: The garbageman drags his donkey straight ahead.

EDICT MAKER: NO PERMIT FOR MULES TO GO ON STRIKE. IT IS FORBIDDEN TO KISS.

IT IS ILLEGAL TO THINK, PRAY, GET UP OR SIT DOWN WITHOUT VISA.

IT IS INADVISABLE TO DO THE FOLLOWING:

TO EXPOSE FEET AND EYES TO ANY BUT THIRD COUSINS ON THE MOTHER'S SIDE; TO RETURN THE GAZE OF FOREIGNERS; TO STARE AFTER DEPORTED FOREIGNERS; TO SLEEP UNDER PILES OF OLD NEWSPAPER; TO CONNECT THIS AND THAT WITH SUCH-AND-SUCH AN EVENT OR PLACE OR SITUATION – THAT IS CONCLUSIONS ARE NOT TO BE DRAWN;

TO LOVE, CRY OUT FOR MERCY, ASK FOR FREEDOM, JUSTICE OR DARKER AND MORE NOURISHING BREAD.

DONKEYS UNDER A LOAD OF ICE BLOCKS WOULD BE ILL-ADVISED TO RELAX THEIR HAUNCHES IN FRONT OF BUTCHERS' SHOPS: IT LITTLE BECOMES THE MEEK TO EXPOSE THEMSELVES.

NO BEATNIKS OR STARVING POETS ALLOWED ON THESE SHORES.

IT IS PROHIBITED.

WILL BE SHOT ON SIGHT.

GUARD: STIN IGIA SAS.

O: Can it be proved that martyrdom is an unreality?

A: Are rats eating men, or men rats?

L: (*in a trance, slowly, as if she had been standing for many hours at a mountain monastery night-vigil. Closed eyes, folded arms, relaxed, her body pivoting*) If circling outwards from the ikon where faded the gardenia, the sacristan making sign of sleep hid the flower in my shit-bag, giving to me what had first been given to the virgin, why from her to me? This could be subversion by circling outwards from the wormy panel where the flower, placed so, can be a message. A signal to whom it is difficult to imagine.

A: Among the fat bodies waddling seaward, where could a sign be read as a sign?

GUARD: The sea's warm, plenty to eat, nothing to complain of.

J: Oiled bodies float towards the smiling shark.

A: Irresistible, joyful fate, to be monster-swallowed.

L: The dead whisper with the dead; the living gossip with the dead; the dead speak of loneliness; the living tell the dead of how hard it is to be alive, thereby destroying them a second time.

J: How I disagree. They have the advantage over us. They are quiet, which is wholeness.

(*The* EDICT MAKER *walks off briskly, looking back over his shoulder. As he goes out, the prisoners move forward, following his body with their eyes.*)

Out there among the leaves of the shade-tree the secret police sit thick as locusts, munching our reputations.

A: Over the rock, past milk-bushes and camel-thorn comes an army of ants in battle formation. Being on the right side of their own laws they advance confidently, predestined to a victorious death.

L: The hands of my son have been crushed. The feet of my son have been torn by whips. The lips of the sea suck the mothering shore. Water is radiant when stars touch it, where whitebait jump. The moon has fallen down the sky at the back of mountains we shall never be allowed to know.

J: Tell me, guard, aren't the windows of our camp like a small village from the other side of the bay?

A: We had a clearer idea of what conditions would be like when we were still a day and night's ship journey away from here.

(*Prisoners retreat.* GUARD *goes away after looking into each cage, particularly the empty number 4. A sound of chains.*)

A: The key has been turned, and yet, how strange! I am less a prisoner than when I feared capture.

O: You there, next door, can you hear me?

A: I can smell you. We both stink the same, probably.

O: Why are you laughing?

A: I didn't laugh; just clearing my throat.

O: You have a wintry cough, though it's only the beginning of autumn.

A: Stop joking. Don't say anything, if you can't be serious.

O: Poor chap! Were you never teased before? I'll lie down on my bed, then you can forget me.

A: Please! Don't go away. I like the sound of your breathing.

O: How old are you?

A: I've no memory for dates and anniversaries, only for faces and weather. A more interesting question would be, how long do you think we'll be prisoners?

O: We may be freed tomorrow or never, who knows? Least of all the ones who put us here. Will I be alive at the end of the play?

A: This kind of thing never happened to me before, but it is taken for granted that actors and audience leave at the end of the performance.

O: Yes, they go out of the room after they have turned off the lights. The weather will be changeable, blowing now hot, now frigid; calm, smiling, tempestuous, sullen.

O: Be careful. The Guard is outside, listening to us.

A: Yes . . . Do you agree that certain days are hot, while others are cold?

O: You are extremely polite. Is your head small?

A: I'd show you the shape of it, if I could get at you. CLOWN!

O: How easily we forget our audience. Yes, it must be little and shaped like a peardrop.

A: I often wondered what it would be like, to be in prison. Hardship draws men together, they used to tell me, but that was theory. Experience would have taught them to be less philosophical. If we are still side by side in ten years' time, despair will probably have made us like twin apples. I simply want to be left in peace to try and understand the present situation. All you can think of is to ask me how old I am and whether my head is small. Question yourself, not me.

O: I can't see far, or hear too well. When I ask questions –

A: You are saying: don't leave me alone.

O: Big liar.

A: Little angel.

O: Little angel.

A: Big liar.

(GUARD *comes in.*)

GUARD: Hold your tongue. It is forbidden to speak in code.

O: Corporal, slope arms! I shall be speechless.

A: I was talking to myself.

O: So was I . . . but, since you ask, I do want a little water.

GUARD: Your type always asks for water.

O: Let me alone, animal trainer!

(GUARD *goes out. Prisoners come forward, except for* Z.)

A: It has happened. I have forgotten how.

O: (*quickly*) I remember why.

L: (*quickly*) Tell me who. Show me what.

GUARD: (*off-stage, terribly, as from a dry well*) It is forbidden.

L: (*quickly*) It doesn't matter now. I remember where.

(Prisoners, except for Z, come forward, moving with violence, jerking their arms and legs.)

J: I was born
to have
to be
to drink
to sleep.

A: I was born
to see
to hear
to speak
to read.

L: I was born
to do
to arrive
to remain
to depart.

O: I was born
to begin
to know
to give
to take.

J: I was born
to learn
to be able to die.

O: I need water
When will the custodian come back?
Where does that road go?

J: Straight on;

left; right;
go on; stop.

O: Have you a map, anyone?
Is there a guide amongst us?
We need a guide
who has the key;
Do you know the way?
How many hours' walk?

A: To the north.

L: To the south.

O: To the east.

A: To the west.

O: (*meditatively*) A sheltered cove and a boat with oars forgotten at the rowlocks.

A: Only a fool leaves oars in a boat.

O: Blessings on the head of that man, whoever he may be.

J: A baling can, a fishing-line, tarpaulins, a lug sail, a tin of bait.

L: A moonless night, a following wind.

O: And fresh water.

J: We'd need a lot of luck not to be picked up either on the beach or just as we were pushing out the boat. They so often lay traps at sea level.

(*Footsteps in the distance.*)

O: The Guard is coming back. I hope the water is going to be cold.

(GUARD *comes in, carrying a round tin tray suspended from chains. There are only four glasses; he hands water to each prisoner except* O.)

O: I was the one who asked.

GUARD: (*goes to one side, begins to read newspaper*) End of today's lesson.

A: You must learn to be more discreet. Don't you remember, you called him 'animal trainer'?

O: It'll be 'goat fucker' next time, see if it isn't.

A: The vanity of martyrs! No wonder you are parched with thirst. Your throat must be full of ashes.

O: Queen of faggots! Whoremaster! Let them cut out my tongue.

A: How sad, to think your mother never taught you the facts of life.

L: (*turning towards* Z) One can never be certain; only try to do one's best for a child. When I taught him to tell the truth, do you think I had any idea of where I was sending him to?

A: There are men out there, walking freely because they signed the necessary documents. They are the dead. Mourn them, not your son.

ALL: (*with upturned glasses emptied of water*) VIVE LA MORT!

J: What a performance! Here we are, huddled together under the bright electric lights, keeping stiff lips, bearing up like refugees, being ugly together, braced against the anonymous Generals: the sick getting sicker, going where?

L: After they had taken him away, I began to lose memory of certain events, was busy with needle and thread sewing buttons on lips, stitching tongue to cheek.

A: Congratulations!

L: Don't mention it.

A: Speak lower, not slower.

GUARD: (*throws away the newspaper, walks nervously up and down*) Is this a gathering of five people? If so, it is a crime against the state. Therefore, you are guilty.

O: Punishment on punishment. We're in jail and it's still not enough.

L: (*turning her head in the direction of O's voice*) I have lost a mind in black wastes. Can you help me understand what happens when the brain runs away into the desert?

O: My name is . . .

A: Better not say it aloud.

L: Can't somebody find what I've mislaid, carve symbols on the chest of family bones so that I may regain ancestry?

(GUARD *goes out with tray of emptied glasses.*)

O: (*comes forward*) Water! I still can't believe they do such things in front of witnesses.

A: Don't be a fool. We are prisoners, not testifiers. It's time you learned to accept what has happened.

O: Water! Why didn't any of you plead for me? Were you afraid?

A: He gave me a drink.

O: Whose side are you on, theirs or ours?

A: My own.

J: Try to rise above the situation. We walk into their traps when we bicker among ourselves.

O: I give up. (*Retreats to the back of the cage.*)

J: Let's pretend it's August, not quite too late for hope. To keep sane, we have to invent our own lives. So, because there's (shall we say) a woman with me and a neighbour might see us through the mosquito net, I'm going to turn out the lights and close the shutters. What relief to lie down, though the mattress is burning-damp from the humid night.

O: Is the last of summer the end of hope?

J: If we haven't been rescued by the end of the dog days, there's not much chance before next spring.

A: Shall I ever be free to say, thanks be to God, I am over the watershed?

O: If only I could believe it was only a game.

J: But why not say it's not yet too late in the year? This girl I'm with doesn't speak. I can hear her heart beating, it's so still in our dark house. (*Intimately to* L) Do you know how she came to me? Through the cinnamon-fragrant night, carrying a bowl of goat's milk, a bunch of parsley in the pocket of her skirt.

Yesterday, the vine stock was a mouldy twig; today it is covered with leaves and tendrils.

We fall asleep. I wake up. Cocks are crowing in the hollow dawn, and the girl is speaking to herself.

L: (*in a high voice, hysterically*) Love and embrace the dwellers in remote gardens, who know the south wind of springtime, the south wind of desire, who pick the young almond, soft to the touch and taste, who tolerate uncompliant children, who savour the smell of clean washing. (*In her normal voice*) Lemon, venetian vetches; orchis, fritillary. How hard to remember an olive tree when the soul is behind bars.

(*The prisoners come forward and look through the bars of their cages, trying to invoke images of an olive tree. Z does not move forward. He sits on a stool in the corner of his cage in the attitude of a performing dog or lion, next to the inside wall of A's cage. A for the first time becomes aware of this 'man next door'. Prisoners come forward, all save Z, who remains seated on stool.*)

A: This person who is too silent on the other side of the wall, nursing grudges in his cell of honeycomb, at any moment will begin to scream. He's holding his belly, an indication of hysteria.

L: Besides, look at his eyes: they are crossed like a spiteful cat's.

Z: Quick, slowly, up, down, in, out.

A: He is going to spew the beans on which he has lived without much complaint against the seeing eye.

Z: Who, where, which, what? When, how?

L: He can trust nobody, so he has to cry out his frightful message without opening his lips.

Z: Near? Far. Early? Late. Always? Never. God on the right side, the Devil on the other. I'm afraid to be touched, through not knowing which way God or the Devil may decide to jump.

(Z *suddenly leaps up and in one bound is at the bars which he clutches until his hands whiten. The others respond to his frenzy and also come forward.*)

L: There's been an accident. Call the doctor and the hospital.

Z: I need injections for rabies and snakebite. I feel sick; it may be typhoid. I cut myself – blood – it is bleeding.

O: It's necessary to be vaccinated, to drink only distilled water, to be wrapped in layers of cotton wool, to wear bandages over the eyes.

L: Send for iodine, disinfectant, insecticide. Cauterise! Cauterise!

Z: I have blisters. Inject me through a glass – give me dark glasses.

L: There should be remedy in liquid or in powder form.

Z: There must be a clinic against mortality.

L: There's been an accident. Record it in the language of tongues. Translate it carefully.

J: It's urgent to have communication.

Z: I need a penknife and sealing-wax. Can you telephone? Write the number down. Ring me up. For Christ's sake, leave a message.

(*The* EDICT MAKER *returns with the* GUARD *and prisoner* H.)

EDICT MAKER: Let me consider. Yes, I have the solution. Lock him in between Z and L.

GUARD: Sir.

A: A brilliant mind. Nothing else to do; unless you put him in with one of us, which would be unorth –

GUARD: Forbidden!

L: I think there's been an accident in cage three.

A: Yes, it happened suddenly. He'd not spoken before, when –

EDICT MAKER: Enough of this. Silence! What's going on?

H: I beg you – just a moment. Before you shut me up, may I look in from outside to see what it's like? It interests me to know your viewpoint, too.

GUARD: (*switches on the light in cage 4, then locks door on* H) Get inside, you bastard.

EDICT MAKER: IT IS FORBIDDEN:

FOR CHILDREN TO PICK WILD FLOWERS ON SUNDAY MORNINGS;

to break glasses and plates, arms, legs and other bones in places of public entertainment;

TO COMMENT ON THE PREVALENCE OF POLICEMEN;

to criticise the man with the briefcase;

TO PUT MESSAGES IN BOTTLES AND COMMIT THEM TO THE SEA;

to read, write or think without reference to the authorities;

to complain of cockroaches in the rice.

L: There's been an accident in cage three.

EDICT MAKER: IT IS FORBIDDEN:

FOR THE CHILDREN OF FEMALE PRISONERS TO REMAIN WITH THEM;

for the children to misbehave because of this;

for the mothers to complain because of this.

Z: (*beats round the walls of his cage with flat palms, then begins to scream*) Blood! Blood! Death is bleeding me! The things I have seen . . . Give me a gun, you there!

O: He's foxing. It's quite a well-known trick.

EDICT MAKER: Silence. Is this a mad-house?

(*Pause. The* EDICT MAKER *goes forward, puts a hand between the bars of the cage, touches Z on the left shoulder.*)

Z: Aaahh! Aaahh! The Devil, the Devil! I burn, I burn!

(*The* EDICT MAKER *leaps away, shaking his hand as if he has received an electric shock.*)

GUARD: Sir, be careful, the beasts can never be trusted.

L: Haven't you any sense? Can't you see he's sick?

Z: (*begins to remove his clothes from the feet up*) First, my Easter boots. Haven't taken them off for a long time, not since the soldier tickled my throat with our breadknife.

L: When was that, son?

Z: Who are you? Are you my mother?

L: No, my boy was done to death. Habit made me call you son.

Z: *Justus ut palma florebit; sicut cedrus Libani multiplicabitur in domo Domini.*

EDICT MAKER: What's he saying?

L: The innocent man will flourish as the palm tree flourishes: he will grow to greatness in the Lord's house as the cedars grow on Lebanon.

GUARD: IT IS FORBIDDEN TO SPEAK FOR –

EDICT MAKER: Hold your tongue, block! *I* am the EDICT MAKER.

Z: . . . *ludens in orbe terrarum; et deliciae meae esse cum filiis hominum.*

L: . . . made play in this world of dust, with the sons of Adam for my playfellows.

Z: Now, the trousers.

H: Why are you taking your pants down? Is *that* why you're inside?

O: I wish I could see what's going on. A, what's he doing?

A: Removing his lower garment.

O: You make it sound like holy ritual.

Z: . . . *mea culpa, mea culpa, mea maxima culpa.*

L: . . . through my fault, through my own fault, through my most grievous fault.

EDICT MAKER: I understand.

O: Water! Water!

GUARD: Sir, I remember why I asked you to return to this section: under ruling 11.5, five people gathered together –

EDICT MAKER: Yes, yes, I know my own pronouncements, thank you.

GUARD: There are six of them now.

O: I demand a glass of water.

A: That's no way to get what you want.

H: Have you been here long, you others?

J: None of us can remember. After the first week, it felt like eternity.

O: How you exaggerate. They brought us from the ship within the past hour.

J: My sense of time must be different from yours.

Z: (*removing his tunic*) Such pressure from clothes: the shirt was like a stone on my heart.

A: Surely, he stinks more than the rest of us put together.

EDICT MAKER: He's playing into our hands. If he takes off his underpants and vest, we'll have to act at once.

H: You can't accuse a man of indecent exposure within the confines of his cage.

EDICT MAKER: We have power to accuse you of anything at any time.

L: Can't you see our point of view?

Z: *Quomodo potest homo nasci, cum sit senex? numquid potest in ventrem matris suae iterato introire, et renasci?*

L: He said: How is it possible that a man should be born when he is already old? Can he enter a second time into his mother's womb, and so come to birth?

A: Guard! This man next to me needs water.

Z: (*shrieks. With his heavy boots he smashes the light-bulb overhead*) They can see me; all of them – the men, the woman too, in league with devils. I heard them sniffing round the door like wolves. Save me, darkness! (*He tries to fasten trousers and tunic across the bars of the cage.*)

EDICT MAKER: Guard, arrest that man.

O: How original he is! Small wonder they made him maker of edicts. Where can they put Z now?

(*The* GUARD *unlocks gate of cage 3. Z almost falls from weakness as he comes forward. He recoils from the light. The* EDICT MAKER *grips him expertly with a policeman's clutch, being careful to hold him by the right shoulder, remembering his previous mistake.*)

Z: How good to feel your hand. God likes a man who strokes his fur the right way. Why won't they give me a gun? You are my friend; give me a gun or a stick, then I'll soon settle these bastards.

H: I hope this cage can't be broken into.

L: He's shaking with terror. Why don't you give him soup?

A: And while you are at it, water for my friend here.

Z: (*whining, vaguely conscious of repeating himself*) God on the right side, the Devil on the other. I'm afraid to be touched, through not knowing which way God or the Devil may decide to jump.

EDICT MAKER: (*to* GUARD) Bring two chairs.

Z: (*falls to his knees and begins to gabble words from the Roman Missal*) *IN NOMINE PATRIS, ET FILII, ET SPIRITUS SANCTI, AMEN . . . et quare tristis incedo, dum affligit me inimicus?*

(*The* EDICT MAKER *points his index finger at* L's *mouth.*)

L: IN THE NAME OF THE FATHER AND OF THE SON, AND OF THE HOLY GHOST, AMEN . . . why do I go mourning, with enemies pressing me hard?

Z: (*censing the air with an imagined thurible*) *Dirigatur, Domine, oratio mea sicut incensum in conspectu tuo; elevatio manuum mearum sacrificium vespertinum.*

J: Welcome as incense-smoke, let my prayer rise up before thee, Lord; when I lift up my hands, be it as acceptable as the evening sacrifice.

(*There is a smell of incense.*)

EDICT MAKER: Bring the woman out! Fetch another chair.

(*The* GUARD *releases* L *and switches off light in cage 5. He goes out for chair.*)

L: As old as my father'd have been, if he'd lived.

Z: (*flings himself at the* EDICT MAKER *who, taken aback, retreats a little*) Don't let them get me! (*Pointing back to cages, whispering to the audience.*) They want to kill me, those people back there. I have no merchandise; my personal effects are hanging on the bars of the grille. To be on the safe side, let's apply for rubber stamps, permits, peanuts, passes, piss-pots, visas, identity cards, false noses, tarot cards.

(*The* GUARD *returns with chair, which he places near the* EDICT MAKER.)

Z: (*becoming more involved, because the audience is not visible as individuals; kneeling down*) Come to me if you need information, residence permits (free passes to *eisteddfodau*), or a guide to the ruins. Would you like to drop in at the embassy for morning coffee, or to meet a tattered consul who can cure the pox? I enjoy the friendship of certain aristocratic ministers of state, none of them less than six feet tall, most of whom are willing to bend an ear occasionally to requests from recommended persons. (*Pointing*) You want a work permit? When did it expire? Renew it. It has to be stamped. (*To another*) You need to apply, to declare, to sign, countersign, rubber-stamp the rubber-stamp of the interpreter in the customs house. (*To another*) Examine currency at the controls. (*To another*) You are an alien. Your face needs endorsement. (*To another*) Bloody foreigner, I'd like to examine your baggage. (*To another*) Your birthplace, profession, great-great grandparents' nicknames, nationality, religion, the sick inventions. (*To another*) If you want a bedroom in the tourist pavilion, I have boys fresh from the Orient. It's not illegal. Say the word, and it's done. (*Rises on one knee; shrieks, pointing at* L.) WIDOW, THIS IS FOR YOU. *En ipse stat post parietem nostrum, respiciens per fenestras, prospiciens per cancellos . . . Sicut balsamum aromatizans . . . myrrha electa . . .*

L: And now he is standing on the other side of this very wall; now he is looking through each window in turn, peering through every chink . . .

J: Cinnamon and odorous balm . . .

EDICT MAKER: (*to the* GUARD, *pointing at cage 6, J's cell*) Unlock that one. I want to study him more closely. (*Pointing downwards, as J comes out*) You can sit on the floor.

(J *sits down close to Z, who draws back his lips and snarls at J. J moves further off.*)

EDICT MAKER: CAREFUL, EVERYBODY. (*To Z*) Stand up or sit down on this chair. Kneeling is for nuns and priests.

Z: I am a priest.

O: Unfrocked!

A: Defrocked?

O: To be able to gabble Latin proves nothing. It's an old confidence trick used by vagrants on pious spinsters. He'd rather be in a straitjacket than in a condemned cell, that's clear.

H: You out there, how does it feel?

J: Much the same as inside. I can still see bars in front of my face.

GUARD: Sir! Do you realize what they are doing to us? Especially this one, this lunatic?

EDICT MAKER: For the last time, SHUT YOUR MOUTHS. (*Pauses, then turns to J.*) A strong memory?

J: It was always rough weather on Saturday afternoons,

the sea burnished silver. Could a boat live on it, could that boat return?

EDICT MAKER: What do you remember most clearly from the past?

J: A garden, never walked through. It belonged to an old manor, and was dedicated to silence. Cypresses, almond and olive trees were disposed about its shallow terraces. One brown sheep grazed there, always round the same spot. Under the tallest cypress was a stone drinking-trough shaped like a small coffin. After the first rains of autumn, the garden becomes green. The solitary sheep –

EDICT MAKER: Is of no interest to me. (*Turning to* L) What can you offer?

L: The last thing I saw before banishment. As we were waiting to be taken out by tender to the destroyer, a red caïque stood into the bay, and dropped anchor near the dock. Like ripening figs, sponges hung in clusters from her yards. Young men, sinuous-oiled as gods, stood on the deck hungry for boys tremulous as their own images in the water. Nobody on shore except ourselves, the guards and the policemen. Not one beautiful youth –

EDICT MAKER: To interest them or me.

L: But these mercenaries, half-gods of the salt and sun, these divers, these tawny bodies, musky with essence of Asia Minor –

EDICT MAKER: Are of no interest to me, I say. Before I interrogate Z, Guard, take him away. Have his hair cut; shave his beard; find decent clothes for him. I suspect him of being much younger than he wishes to appear.

(*The* GUARD *goes off, Z firmly held by right shoulder.*)

What is that noise?

J: Only our friends the rats moving into the empty cages.

EDICT MAKER: (*aside*) It is rumoured that these creatures are agents of the revolutionaries, carrying information from island to island.

O: (*musing*) The splendour of the moon, the spendthrift stars of the Levant . . . How normal, how singular, to wake in foreign harbours under mountains tawny with pits of old snow; seraphim, and bell-tolling hours in chocolate-perfumed towns.

EDICT MAKER: (*turning to* A) You there, of what are you thinking?

A: Of my father, a killer of vermin.

EDICT MAKER: He was a mole-catcher?

A: No, a hunter of foxes.

O: I can see him, cold and hungry – they never have enough to eat in your valleys.

A: My neck of the world? You don't know where I come from.

O: Your accent gives you away. Isn't it true, you come from a landscape with cataracts?

EDICT MAKER: Was he successful, this sporting father of yours?

A: He had small terriers which he put down the earths. They were true professionals, and loved their life

30

underground, the smell of their quarry in subterranean lairs. As a result of their aptitude, our farmhouse inside and out was hung with fox pelts. My father had many sheep. To be a good flockmaster such as he was, you must be a relentless killer of vermin.

EDICT MAKER: (*turns towards* O) Now you, in the first cage, being so careful to keep out of the limelight, why are you trying to hide from the audience?

O: Whatever I say will be used in evidence against me. I'm lying down, and I don't intend to talk except in front of a judge. In certain circumstances, as I said a short time ago to our custodian corporal guard, I shall be speechless. When I make a harmless request for water, I'm disregarded. When you seek to trap me into saying something that may be harmful to myself and others, I disregard you.

(*The* GUARD *returns, with* Z *looking twenty years younger. Now dressed like the others, his appearance is that of any unremarkable young man. He fingers his freshly-shaven face, as if ashamed of its nakedness.*)

Z: Look at me, a deluded Samson. My hands itch to pull down the pillars of your house.

O: How long is he going to be able to keep up this pretence?

A: Why are you sure it is not the real thing? He looks insane to me, and even more dangerous without his beard.

EDICT MAKER: Sit down. Listen to me carefully. After a certain amount of expensive investigation, it has been established that you are not in fact the character known so far as Z.

Z: Give me medicine. The pain is here, in my arm, in my chest.

EDICT MAKER: Are you a foreign subject?

A: Who isn't?

Z: (*in ordinary voice*) I wish to see the consul.

EDICT MAKER: Certainly, but first tell me the name of your consulate.

Z: Was I born to fill up forms, 30,000 feet above the earth? Was I born to be alienated? Was I born to have a number burned into my arm and brain? To whom shall I apply in order to have my boots cleaned? Must I declare the corpse hidden in my suitcase?

L: Was he conceived, to be wrenched apart in front of my eyes?

Z: If I am not Z, who am I?

EDICT MAKER: It has been discovered who you are not, not who you are, which is a matter for further enquiry. Unless you care to cooperate with us?

H: Since when has torture been known as cooperation?

Z: I am Z, baptized Z, of a father surnamed Z.

EDICT MAKER: There is no such person. You were carrying false papers.

H: Then he has no right to be here! You might as well let him go.

EDICT MAKER: Each one of you is a menace to the state. Z most of all.

A: Why? For the sake of argument, why is he more dangerous than I am?

EDICT MAKER: Because he sees sparrows as eagles, and can convince you that he has seen them. (*To the* GUARD) Bring the black dossier, if it has been completed. And the branding iron.

(*The* GUARD *goes out. Extreme tension. Each is busy with his own fears.*)

O: Samson Z, I'm afraid it's the pillars of your own house you've pulled down, not his.

A: Do any of you remember being born? My birthright –

O: His birthright –

A: Was in an easier time, before the sun exploded. It was evening of one of those days (they told me later) – cool, damp, grey, trying to rain, the first darkness coming – when they rode out, the black-skinned man on the first mule, the pregnant woman on the second animal, on their way to the summer grazing grounds. The body of my mother on the saddle excited me, and I decided it was time to see more of life. I struggled; she fell from the mule onto a small bush, and so saved us both. I can remember the first smell of crushed myrtle-boughs, the shock of being outside one shelter and into another skin as if it had happened last night, or would happen tomorrow.

(*The* GUARD *comes in carrying a large black folder and a branding iron. He hands the dossier to the* EDICT MAKER, *who runs his right forefinger down several columns in the middle of the book. He speaks as he searches.*)

EDICT MAKER: What was the General doing? Was he busy? Was he angry at being disturbed?

GUARD: He said it mustn't happen again.

EDICT MAKER: Why, what was he doing?

GUARD: Reading the private memoirs of the Dictator.

EDICT MAKER: Give this person his new identity.

(*The* GUARD *brands Z on the left forearm.*)

Z: AAAAAHHHHHHH!

(*He falls shrieking to the floor, clutching his arm.*)

EDICT MAKER: You are no longer Z, but number 295620.

L: (*kneeling, takes Z into her arms, rocks him to and fro*) Weep, you must weep. It eases the pain.

Z: Don't touch me. You are unclean.

L: (*leaps up in horror at his disgust, and backs away from him*) The world withers and blows away. So that was the meaning of it, the fury, the pretence of insanity – a mask to fool me.

Z: Such guilt I feel towards women!

L: Guilt breeds hatred. Nothing is simple any more. Many years ago, my husband complained of me, 'She used to be so clear.' The years pass; so does innocence.

O: Take away my thirst.

EDICT MAKER: (*to the* GUARD) Unlock H, and bring him here.

H: I refuse to come out. This cell I make my church. I claim sanctuary. (*Pointing at* Z) That man is dangerous.

Z: (*fingering his right forearm*) *Vide humilitatem meam.*

(L *turns away her head, showing she will no longer interpret for him.*)

Z: (*going towards her*) Hide me under your downy armpit.

(L *retreats before him, to cage 1. O takes her hand, through the grille.*)

EDICT MAKER: The rules I have made, broken at every turn. It must be part of a new conspiracy, this time a plot within the walls. Prisoners touching one another, refusing to obey orders, talking among themselves in riddles to which they alone know the answers!

(*The* GUARD, *who has hesitated, now goes to unlock the door of* H's *cell.* H *holds the door from the inside, and since he is the stronger of the two, succeeds in keeping it closed.*)

Z: Give me a gun! Shoot out the lights!

L: Why do you persecute me? How do you know?

EDICT MAKER: Guard, put this creature back into her cage. Bring out O and A: they may be needed.

(*The* GUARD *unlocks O and A and goes to lock up L. As they pass one another, O puts his head on her breast.*)

O: For once, I agree with you, maker of edicts. (*To* L) It's best for you to be in there. It's uncomfortable, but you'll be safe, at least safer than it may become out here. If Z is acting a part, it can prove more serious than if he were really out of his mind.

L: God keep you.

O: Naples, Stockholm, London, Stuttgart.

L: I find difficulty in following –

O: Paris, Stamboul.

L: Do you mean, afterwards? . . . Is it ill luck to meet with a corpse in a narrow place?

EDICT MAKER: (*to the* GUARD) I'm going to try a dangerous experiment. We'll leave them on their own for a while: H and L locked up, the others free to move outside the cages. In this way, we can perhaps find out more about them than by interrogation.

(*The* EDICT MAKER *and the* GUARD *go out.*)

Z: A stupid man, in a time of bad weather –

J: Dropped a coin and started a war.

Z: A napkin left in an armchair by a servant –

A: Caused a king to smile, and give up drinking.

Z: My father sent me to a private school. He had a lot of money, which he spent on my education.

(*Pause: they listen.*)

O: You seem proud of it.

(*Pause.*)

A: I think it's safe.

Z: Do you remember me?

O: I have been observing you for a long time.

A: I have been following you for a long time.

Z: I can't do it. I'm afraid of becoming really mad.

J: What could he do on his own?

A: Ultimately, each of us is solitary.

O: So, I was right! He is working for his own ends.

Z: Let me alone. Who are you to judge my motives? I'm my own pilot on this particular course.

A: Have you the chart with quicksands and currents marked, or do you put a blind trust in this God of yours?

Z: I'm allowed to make certain decisions on my own authority – of course, always within the framework of the organisation.

O: It was a lie, when you said you were a priest, wasn't it?

(H *quietly opens the door of his cage and walks out, leaving the door wide open.*)

J: How?

H: When the guard unlocked the door, and I held it shut on the other side, he 'forgot' to relock it. Strange what a difference it makes to walk when I choose, and not when the Edict Maker chooses. It makes me feel almost like a man again.

L: Except that you can't see the sky, the island, or the sea.

A: It's time to consider the position. We now have five empty cages, one of which is unlocked. We might be able to use that fact, before we're through.

O: The last thing I'd have believed possible is that the Edict Maker should leave us alone in this way. It's against the rules of the game. I don't trust it.

J: It's clever – if it's only stopped Z from his raving.

O: (*going to* L's *cell window*) Did you know Z in the old days?

L: I thought I'd be certain after they shaved his beard, but I'm less sure. His face looks naked now and too young to be his. A bearded man is not the same person close-shaven. I'd believed I couldn't feel any more. It was the truth when I said –

O: 'Buttoned and stitched and closed'?

L: It begins again. There is never an end. Nothing ever finishes. We flow like wine, generation into generation, not dying: flow and break down into new shapes, new forms out of archaic moulds.

I love he loves she loves they love.

I die he dies she dies they die, but it is not death: it is the flower in the rock, the bird on the winter sea.

O: Is it night? My eyes are bad. I can't see in the dark. I am almost blind.

L: It is night.

GUARD: (*in the distance*) Listen carefully: the maker of edicts is about to deliver a new pronouncement.

(*The* EDICT MAKER's *voice on loudspeaker, becoming very loud.*)

Our policy is unchanged and will remain unchanged as formulated on the very first day of this glorious revolution. It is a policy of peace, friendship and cooperation. It is forbidden to sing lewd songs in public places. *Paix, amitié, coopération.*

Forbidden Forbidden

Le progrès par l'unité et l'amour.

FORBIDDEN   PROGRESS   POLICY   IMPERMISSIBLE

PROGRESS FORBIDDEN

FORBIDDEN UNITY FORBIDDEN LOVE FORBIDDEN

PROGRESS IS IMPERMISSIBLE FORBIDDEN LOVE PROGRESS

UNITY FORBIDDEN

IT IS DANGEROUS

to recite lewd songs in narrow streets of obscure towns

LOVE.

CHORUS OF VOICES: (*echo, not in unison: obviously a gramophone record, worn with playing*)

. . . of the glorious revolution

as on the *very* first day of that

most glorious revolution. (*Further off – the needle has slipped and is sliding on the record.*)

. . . and so far successful since the *very* first *very* first *very* first *very very very very* glorious revolution . . .

PRISONERS: (*crossing themselves slowly and with elaborate variations*) AMEN.

(*Outside, a rattling of chains.*)

Z: An outsized censer or a new batch of prisoners?

A: (*sniffling*) I smell no incense.

O: If it is new prisoners coming, we'll soon smell them.

CHORUS: (*the record still playing but the motor running down*) glorious revolution g l o r i o u s   r e v o l u t i o n . . .

Z: (*marking the letter A in the air before his face at the head of the imagined cross*) ALPHA. (*Marking the letter Ω in the air towards the floor at the foot of his cross.*)

J: (*looking across at Z, speaking to* A) There was a boy at my school who used to play-act in that way: said he was trying to find out if God existed or not, by provoking the thunderbolt.

A: The experiment worked?

J: The Lord didn't answer.

A: What became of the lad?

J: I don't have a clue. For all I know to the contrary, he may be Z. I saw him only once again, briefly, a year or two after we had both left school. He was white-cuffed, wore a long fingernail (Z *studies his fingernails, all of which are long and dirty*) and was standing under the clock on the number 4 platform at the central station. I told him how tired he looked, and he smiled and said 'I'm waiting, in case he turns up.'

L: My son used to do the same thing . . . stand for hours under that clock, waiting, like a prostitute! More often than not, the other man failed to come.

O: Enough to make the hands stop.

Z: He never came. That's why I decided to go it alone.

EDICT MAKER: (*walking down centre aisle, from back of auditorium*) Now I am Dick, the plain-clothes tec on the prowl, shadowing these dubious characters. Pick-up, antennae well out, a loaf of bread, a newspaper: perfect disguise.

A: *Not* subtle.

EDICT MAKER: The experiment is beginning to work; after this, I'll probably be made personal adviser to the General. (*To the right wings, hoping to make the* GUARD *hear offstage*) Guard, are you there? What the hell are you doing? Reading the newspaper again, I suppose.

GUARD: (*idles on, in an abstracted mood*) What should we do?

EDICT MAKER: Nothing, for the present.

GUARD: Please Sir, what time is it?

EDICT MAKER: Not early. Late, if anything.

GUARD: Then, Sir, with your permission, I'll patrol the beach for a while.

O: What could he do on his own?

EDICT MAKER: I wonder if you are hiding anything from me?

J: Why not?

EDICT MAKER: So, you are leaving? Do as you like, but be careful to look after each gate and door. And remember, once up and down the foreshore will be enough.

GUARD: Sir. (*Goes out briskly.*)

(*The* EDICT MAKER *wanders up the aisle, hands at his back, trying to intimidate members of the audience by staring at them.*)

Z: I hate.

J: What? Who?

Z: I hate.

(*A hollow sound of gates and doors being unlocked and relocked, keys clashing together, into the distance.*)

H: I've a sister and a brother.

J: My uncle has black hair.

O: (*putting on a foreign accent*) At this time, he is in the aeroplane.

A: Shit and fuck!

Z: Stand further off, stinking lump of impotence! If I had a swordfish, I'd use it on you! Shred you small. For sweet Mary's sake, don't lose your nerve at this stage. Do you want the play to end now?

O: So much play on play. It is easier to act a part than to live it.

J: Tact won't solve anything.

A: Just as violence won't, you cretin.

O: *Mou aresei na kolympo me to feggari.*

A: You do it on purpose! I'll kill you, before we're through, I swear to God I will. You always manage to turn the screws on misery. Forgetfulness is the only weapon of any use to us these days.

H: (*going back towards cage 4*) It's my temperament, to keep within my house gate, the windows open but the grilles firm, so that the groping fingers of blind beggars shall not find me. Being inside is preferable to being with you lot. Wake me up at six!

A: I must say, you're a great help.

H: Being theatrical, huddling together in the middle of a stage, isn't the only way to be of use.

A: 'In our predicament . . .'

H: (*bowing*) 'In our predicament . . .'

(*Z is sitting cross-legged on the floor, restlessly fingering the number stamped on his arm. He mutters indistinctly. He crosses himself at intervals.*)

H: Do you think the Guard is keeping his side of the bargain?

J: He's a cool operator, and there's no risk in patrolling a beach and looking into a dinghy.

H: I don't mean that. He might decide not to play along with us – take out the bung or crack a couple of planks in her bottom.

O: Pigs might fly! Take no risks, get no cake.

(*The* EDICT MAKER *is heard, pacing slowly.*)

A: The EDICT MAKER's coming! (*Pause*) A cold wind seems to be blowing in from the sea.

H: (*as the* EDICT MAKER *enters, frowning, preoccupied*) This man strikingly resembles my father. He used to drink in order to forget my mother's existence.

(*The* GUARD *is heard returning. Gates and doors are opened and shut – bolts, chains, keys. He enters.*)

GUARD: A quiet night on the beach, Sir.

EDICT MAKER: Not too quiet?

GUARD: Normally peaceful, Sir.

EDICT MAKER: No shadows on the sea? No footprints at the tide's edge?

L: 'Clawmarks of small birds in black sand.'

EDICT MAKER: So, the seascape was a little unnatural, slightly abnormal?

GUARD: Sir, you are putting words into my mouth.

EDICT MAKER: Why be so sensitive after a routine patrol of the shore?

GUARD: Do I seem nervous, Sir? Perhaps. It could have been the silence down there.

(*The prisoners are anxiously walking round the* EDICT MAKER *and the* GUARD, *as if watching a sparring match.*)

EDICT MAKER: For a warder, your reactions are inappropriate. I wish to speak to you in private. Tomorrow, I shall be in my office from ten in the morning till five in the afternoon. You may come any time during those hours.

GUARD: Sir.

EDICT MAKER: In the meantime, watch your step.

(*The* EDICT MAKER *goes out. As soon as they consider it safe, the three prisoners A, O, and J crowd round the* GUARD. *H has remained in his cage; Z is still on the floor.*)

A, O, J: Well?

GUARD: The boat is there, anchored a short way off shore. Nobody is on the beach at this time of night. There's a tank of fuel, food, water, a lug-sail, fishing line and bait.

O: What about oars?

GUARD: There are oars. Everything has been thought of. Why did I reject my opportunity out there, in the dark? I could, I should have, thrown myself from the cliff into the sea, on the black night wind, while the drum beat was strong in my ears.

(*The* EDICT MAKER *comes back unexpectedly, walking with extreme tension.*)

EDICT MAKER: I AM THE EDICT MAKER, second only to the General on this island. Why then, am I so alone? You have one another.

GUARD: You can take pride in the purity of your convictions, Sir, in the certainty of always being in the right.

A: Like ants, whose armies never retreat, for the same reason.

EDICT MAKER: The necessity of thinking up edicts has turned me into a creative artist.

O: Of the order of Saint Stink, first class!

EDICT MAKER: And as such, I bow my head and prepare for a lonely fame.

H: You'll be infamous, never fear.

(*Off-stage, megaphone, the* EDICT MAKER's *recorded voice.*)

FOREIGN POLICY OF THE GOVERNMENT IS UNCHANGED.

O: Look at those two men, the Edict Maker and Z. I suppose you realize their roles are interchangeable?

A: Think it, don't say it. Never state the obvious. Intelligent people don't like it.

45

O: It's true, all the same.

A: When did you realize it?

O: A few moments ago, when Z suddenly shouted 'I hate' and J asked who or what, and Z simply shouted again 'I hate'; it was just like the Edict Maker, with his senseless announcements.

(*Off-stage, megaphone roars – the* EDICT MAKER's *recorded voice.*)

FOREIGN POLICY OF THE GOVERNMENT IS UNCHANGED.

LA POLITIQUE ÉTRANGÈRE DU GOUVERNEMENT RESTE INCHANGÉE TELLE QUE TRACÉE DÈS LES PREMIERS JOURS DE LA RÉVOLUTION.

BONNES BONNES RELATIONS AVEC TOUS LES ÉTATS INDÉPENDAMMENT DES DIFFÉRENCES DE SYSTÈME SOCIAL ET POLITIQUE ET DEMEURE CERTES FIDÈLE FIDÈLE FIDÈLE FIDÈLE À SES ALLIANCES.

EDICT MAKER: My voice comes out rather well over the loudspeaker, you must agree.

GUARD: Especially in French, Sir.

(*Loudspeaker, the* EDICT MAKER's *voice.*)

WE SEE ALL AROUND IN YOUR HAPPY SMILING FACES THE DEEP REGARD YOU HAVE FOR US – UN ACCUEIL SPONTANÉ ET CORDIAL

LES FRUITS D'UN LABEUR INTENSE

À BAS LES RUINES! À BAS LES RUINES!

UNIS UNIS UNIS

ET NOUS AIMANT LES UNS LES AUTRES

ENTRONS DANS L'ARÈNE

POUR EN SORTIR

VICTORIEUX VICTORIEUX VICTORIEUX

UNE NOUVELLE FOIS

LA FOI FIÈRE

LA FOI HEUREUSE.

GUARD: Especially in French, Sir.

O: My thirst has come back!

(*Loudspeaker, the* EDICT MAKER*'s voice.*)

GARDIENS VIGILANTS

DE LA VIE

DE L'HONNEUR

DE LA SÉCURITÉ

DE LA LIBERTÉ

DE L'INTEGRITÉ TERRITORIALE

NEUTRALISER LES ENNEMIS!

NEUTRALISER LES ENNEMIS!

TOUT COMME APOLLON

COMME APOLLON

AVAIT TUÉ À DELPHES

LE PYTHON LE PYTHON LE PY–

POUR CRÉER LA LUMIÈRE.

(*Loudspeaker, chorus.*)

AVEC L'AIDE DE DIEU!

AVEC L'AIDE DE DIEU!

EDICT MAKER: Having my voice immortalised in this way should compensate for everything I've lost, I suppose.

GUARD: It's long been my ambition to have my voice in print. One never knows, in these uncertain days – stranger things than that can come about.

Z: After the soldier threatened to slit my throat I decided it was time to start walking to another town or country.

L: The family breadknife, curved bonehandle?

Z: Brown with long use, greased by sweating hands.

L: He said he was going to finish you off when he took you into the yard.

GUARD: I said I could, not would. It wasn't for me to do anything on my own, simply bring him to my superior officer.

EDICT MAKER: Something will have to be done about –

GUARD: What, Sir?

EDICT MAKER: The rats. Foreign yachtsmen no longer use the harbour because of –

J: Rodents slipping aboard in their sleek winter coats –

48

H: Carrying discreet valises. (*Sing-song, lugubrious voice.*)

O there were rats, rats
Big as pussy-cats.

J: How's this for next season's slogan?

Delectable island, solid rock, no vegetation –
Set in the fucking sea.
Sun for nine months –

O: And you know what that means?

J: Rain for three months –

O: And you know what that means . . .

J: Rats, rocks. Come join us!

L: (*pointing at the* EDICT MAKER) You were that officer. Can you never have done with horror?

Z: (*shouting*) Peace. Friendship. Cooperation.

EDICT MAKER: (*shouting*) *Quid igitur lex?*

A: How naturally it goes, the transformation.

O: My throat's a parrot cage.

L: Have patience, husband.

O: Water!

(*The* GUARD *goes out briefly, returns with a stone water-jar, the contents of which he throws in O's face. The* EDICT MAKER *watches the* GUARD *carefully.*)

GUARD: That's for insulting the flag!

L: Shit-face! Shit-face!

(L *puts her arms through the bars in an attempt to slide the bolt of the door. The* GUARD *takes the revolver from the holster at his hip, strikes her on both wrists. She falls back into the half-darkness of the cell. The light in the cell goes out.*)

O: Put the light on for the woman.

(*The light goes on, then off, on, off, for several seconds, during which time* L *fumbles round the cage with limp arms, coming to terms with the pain. A man's shadow falls onto the stage from the right wings.*)

EDICT MAKER: Who's that fellow lurking in the corridor? Go and see what he wants.

GUARD: It looks to be someone from headquarters, Sir, a man who works close to the General, a kind of unofficial secretary, I think.

EDICT MAKER: Go and find out what he's up to. I don't like people who hang about in the shadows.

(*The* GUARD *goes out, returns at once with a letter, which he hands to the* EDICT MAKER.)

EDICT MAKER: (*reads*) . . . duh our deep sorrow at being deprived duh our deep sorrow at being deprived of a select colleague who from the first moment of the Revolution had placed himself in the service of the Motherland . . . Faith and regret . . . in defence of interests . . . duh . . . sorrow . . . our deep . . . colleague who . . . the select . . . Revolution . . . pushed . . . the departing Edict Maker for reasons of health . . . to offer his valuable services as a special envoy of the government abroad . . . resigned for reasons of health . . . Thursday.

GUARD: It's Thursday night. First quarter of the moon. The

ninth of the month.

(*The* EDICT MAKER's *voice on loudspeaker, distorted – the tape being run too fast.*)

SMILING FACES ALL AROUND US THE DEEP SORROW YOU HAVE FOR AN ELECTED COMRADE WHO IN FRUITFUL LABOUR CONCEIVED SORROWING UNITY IN A NEW TIME OF RUIN IN THE ARENA CASTRATE THE ENEMY LIQUIDATE THE FOE TOUT COMME TOUT COMME APOLLON AVAIT TUÉ À À À À À DELPHES LE P P P P P P PYTHON ON ON ON.

EDICT MAKER: Monstrous! How can anyone dare? – destroy the tape. Who dared do this to me?

Z: (*walking towards the* EDICT MAKER) I'd like to try on your uniform. (*Holding out his right hand*) Passport, visa, ikon – look lively, we don't have the whole night for this rehearsal. The last train goes – (*The others look at their left wrists.*) Besides, there are many among the audience who have children at home, salting their pillows with cries for mama.

GUARD: We'll leave the children out of this, if it's the same to you. None of your wet, white, woolly sentiments being dragged across the matter in hand. It's a grim night where we are, and none of us can take on extra pressures from outside the walls. This is a crisis.

EDICT MAKER: (*clutches Z, feverishly*) Don't let them take me, those people! I have no merchandise. You are now wearing my personal effects. It's a sign of friendship – no, more: blood relationship – to swop clothes. I'm an old hand at strategy; this must simply be a ruse of the man upstairs. Reverses have to be taken calmly.

(*with Z mouthing the words*) I enjoy the friendship of certain aristocratic ministers of state, none of them less than six feet tall, most of whom are willing to bend an ear occasionally to requests from recommended persons.

Z: You'll be lucky.

H: I've been forgotten. Surely, it's time I acted, to justify my coming back into this den. Besides, the rat sitting in the corner has been staring at me for a long time. Perhaps he's a prompter and thinks I've missed my cue. Since we're paid by the line in this profession, I must think of something to say.

(*The* EDICT MAKER *is listening to him suspiciously.*)

H: (*to the* EDICT MAKER) How do you like your new role?

EDICT MAKER: I was never any good at Latin.

Z: Nor was I, but hear enough repeated enough times, and you're stuck with it.

(*Loudspeaker, Z's voice.*)

IT IS FORBIDDEN:

TO SHOW LACK OF CONFIDENCE IN THE NEW REGIME.

TO ALLEGE THAT A REIGN OF TERROR EXISTS.

TO THINK THAT THE PEOPLE ARE NOT HAPPY AND CALM.

(*During this speech, the* GUARD *goes to look into H's cage, wondering what he is doing. As he bends down to look through the bars, H flings open the door with violence, and sends the* GUARD *sprawling. He leaps upon him and succeeds in snatching the revolver from the* GUARD's *holster. The others*

52

freeze at sight of the gun. In the scuffle, the whip is knocked out of the GUARD*'s hand. It now lies, a dead snake, the length of the stage, between the prisoners and* H. *The* GUARD *can now be counted as a prisoner.*)

Z: (*shrieks*) A gun! Give me the gun!

(*Loudspeaker, Z's voice.*)

IT IS FORBIDDEN:

TO SHOW LACK OF CONFIDENCE IN THE NEW REGIME.

TO ALLEGE THAT A REIGN OF TERROR EXISTS.

TO THINK THAT THE PEOPLE ARE NOT HAPPY AND CALM.

H: Which one of you shall I kill first?

L: There's a saying: 'Women and children, last'.

H: The fiery arm – instantaneous control, the one charm that always works. (*Shouts to the distance.*) No need to tape this takeover.

(*A voice on a tape, yelling.*)

A REIGN OF TERROR EXISTS.

THE PEOPLE ARE NOT HAPPY OR CALM.

LACK OF CONFIDENCE IN THE NEW REGIME.

EDICT MAKER: Bravo! Bravo! (*to the* GUARD) What's become of the secret police? Why aren't they out there in the tree, keeping an eye on things? They could easily shoot this traitor in the back.

Z: It's getting late, and they've had a long day. They're asleep already, snoring round the roots.

EDICT MAKER: In that case, they'll be stark mad by morning.

H: Into your cages!

(*A circus fanfare. Using the revolver as a magnet,* H *draws first the* EDICT MAKER *and* Z *into cage 1, having taken the keys from the* GUARD. H *locks them in. Comes back for the* GUARD, *whom he locks in cage 3. He puts* A *in cage 5 with* L; O *in cage 2;* J *in cage 4.*)

L: I've strong teeth to bite you with: long nails to tear out your eyes. Get to hell, away from me. You smell of the dungheap.

A: Go on, go on, weep your turtle tears. You please me, randy widow; your rage excites me. Where there's anger, there's passion of another sort.

O: Who wants to be loved by moonlight, and the sound of pipes?

L: I do.

H: (*beating time to the music with the revolver*) This is how it should have been from the beginning, but the Director thought otherwise.

L: How is it going to end?

H: So far, I haven't a clue, but we'll work it out between us. Don't force things. Let it happen naturally.

O: (*mocking*) Play it cool, man, play it cool.

H: (*begins to sing, extravagantly, narrowing his eyes, shading them with a hand; then, with light touches of fingers, making*

the mime of putting on handcuffs and crying out defiantly)
What's become of the police? (*Inserting words into the music, repeating them several times, with passion*) Rats, rats, big as pussy cats, in the Edict Maker's bed. (*In an attempt to cheer himself up*)

There are rats, rats
Big as pussy cats
In the Edict Maker's cell.

(*Shouts*) Now I can take my time over studying what it's like from outside, looking in.

(*The music breaks off abruptly.*)

GUARD: What price, escape?

H: God, what a lovely place life is!

J: May I quote a deleted passage from near the end of my fourth forthcoming book? 'So passed the days and nights, the men digging escape tunnels that ended in the next cell, or the next-but-one cell block or in a flooded sewer or before the grille of a confession box; the rats, their teeth chittering with nervous enthusiasm, gnawed at the corners of the walls or at the legs of the prisoners.'

H: Why was it taken out?

J: The publishers thought it showed too little optimism.

Z: I know how I'd like to end it.

A: End what?

Z: This.

A: I know how you'd end it, coward. Say it was a dream,

go so far as to say it's allegorical, that dirty word! Say it was a myth.

H: How can anyone foretell his end? Age brings no wisdom. The sun confused me when I lay under him, for he burned away dross like a fired needle, leaving only the sun. Now, his absence shakes me.

Z: Let us try to detach ourselves from the area of pain.

(*Loudspeaker, an advertisement.*)

Try it in your lavatory – untouched by human hand:

RAT POISON invented by rats, for rats.

The most hygienic method so far discovered for the extermination of your dependent friends and enemies. Try it today. Large free samples, enough to kill one hundred souls without mess, fuss or danger to the user – in Lilac Green; Utility Grey; Erotic Black; cartons that youngsters will find irresistible; bumper size; family size; suisize.

J: Nobody could say the situation was ideal. They've started to advertise; the end of pure art.

H: I can't do it. It's no use trying to act out of character: it fools nobody. The gun isn't my property, after all. I felt at home immediately in the cage, knew my limits. If I shot the others, it would hardly help *me*. I know I couldn't face the sea alone in a small boat.

O: L, where are you? Suddenly, it's as if you were out of my life. A, if there is anything going on, if you lay your hands on her, you'll have to meet me afterwards. I warn you now.

A: Shall I tell you something interesting? You should take a good look at her, as I am doing. She's no heroic matron: this is a woman full of sap, and too young to have a grown-up son.

Z: (*tenderly to* L) . . . *myrrha, et gutta, et casia a vestimentis tuis* . . .

L: . . . myrrh, aloes, cassia . . .

Z: . . . *decore Indis florescere voluisti* . . .

L: . . . should blossom in the far Indies . . .

GUARD: To speak in code now is senseless.

EDICT MAKER: A last bid for sympathy –

GUARD: From those people out there in the half-darkness.

H: House lights ON for just a moment. I must have a peep into the future. I look everywhere for a sign, I look for signs! (*Glances over the audience.*) GOD! Lights out. (*Screams, pointing to the body of the theatre.*) House lights OUT!

O: The sea is full of hair,
Full of sharp teeth.

L: Long tails stream with the tide.

A: A sea of lifted snouts
Of grey hair.

H: Did I see what I thought I saw, out there in the curve of the painted breakers? Give me the gift of an exotic tongue, fluid words of Africa . . . or sieges of Sumatra, snows of India. O ancient wheel, golden Catherine wheel, your horses trod us into the burning dust. I watch at an improbable hour, while cats scream over the camp, hollow as death. I suffer from too much seeing.

A: My horoscope for today reads:

'Seize opportunity by the breast.'

O, boy: two, full as gourds. The first stroke of luck I've had since, when? In spring, she will be rutting-mad, a maenad, her breasts swollen at the time of almond blossom. In February, the humming of bees, the falling of white blossom. Unnaturally warm, earthquake weather.

L: I hate your hands.

O: I can see and hear you. H, for the love of God, let me out of here, and lend me the gun for a moment. You say you have no use for it. I have, by Jesus.

H: No, it's not the time for melodramatic gestures.

J: Take your own advice: play it cool.

L: So that, with luck, we'll survive the night, and even be of some use afterwards.

EDICT MAKER: I wouldn't mind being the one to tidy up and put out the dustbins.

L: I want to tip up the seats and look for fallen earrings.

A: And then walk out of the stage door, disguised as myself.

Z: Listen! Can you hear that noise in the next cage? It's the Devil scratching the wall. (*Clutching the* EDICT MAKER *by the lapels of his tunic*) Not a sound; if we don't move, he'll think I've gone away. Curse you, forked abomination! (*Falling to his knees, clutching the* EDICT MAKER's *thighs*) Save, charitable doctor; a cure; make me whole! The pain in my chest presses me to the ground.

EDICT MAKER: Here is a phial I was able to smuggle in, the only certain cure for satanophobia. It's full of white angels – see their wings fluttering? Enough for twenty doses. Take one before retiring, and you'll be safe for the night. Trust me, I'm your friend.

Z: They look small. Will they be proof against the monster?

EDICT MAKER: Faith is half the cure.

O: (*tapping the wall*) Here, you two, what's going on?

EDICT MAKER: We find we have much in common.

Z: Don't speak of me. Pretend you are alone.

EDICT MAKER: Nobody but me. Number 295620 has been spirited away.

Z: See how long I can hold my breath when the Devil's abroad!

O: Who's there with you, if it isn't Z?

EDICT MAKER: I indulge in double talk.

O: Like this double agent next to me, the swine with two faces.

GUARD: Whose hand are you playing but your own, same as me? Where's the difference?

J: I don't believe this is happening in reality. It keeps reminding me of something I wrote a while back. My publishers were shocked by it, said they thought if that was the effect the place had on my work, I should try making a home somewhere else. They didn't know it was already too late for me to get out. I remember their words: 'If you are so unhappy and sick at heart, couldn't you find another island? There are many of them.'

A: The last comfort gone. I had hoped there was only this one.

L: We are on.

Z: I hate.

(*Loudspeaker, Z's voice.*)

. . . *la mission de sauver la jeunesse de l'immoralité et de la corruption.*

Des objectifs éducatifs et culturels d'une foule anarchiste, à préparer des ennemis de la patrie à pousser beaucoup de jeunes à la misère, l'immoralité et la corruption.

(*Z speaks in his own voice again.*)

Viole un cadavre avec la bénédiction!

(*Loudspeaker, Z's voice.*)

L'immoralité et la corruption.

EDICT MAKER: I hate.

Z: We are afraid. We are held. We are lost. I am afraid. I was examined. I'm a number. I forget what it is.

H: They are the lucky ones. Each with a snug roof, firm walls, sound floor, a front door –

J: With a lock on it.

H: And a bed, while I'm out here without anything to sleep on.

A: You've the two chairs. Use your ingenuity.

H: Endless corridors, gates, doors, locks.

GUARD: A melancholic beach and desolate wastes of salt water without end, leaping to another far-off shore.

H: And returning –

J: Into the same half-worn body.

GUARD: Into the same encircled mind.

H: Safely inside, you want to be outside, a free agent.

A: Outside, you are an outcast longing for respectability.

L: The boy they took away, the children I could have borne.

O: Had we lived in a less dangerous time.

J: All time is dangerous.

A: As women are. Oh, I know your type, sorceress, casting wide the net but throwing every fish back into the sea as being too small to bother with. What's wrong with me – do I have less to offer than O?

L: There shall be nothing given, nothing taken. It is the end of our time.

A: One can always think up a new means of escape.

L: (*turning violently towards O's cage*) Get out of my dream! What right have you earned to haunt my nights? I swam in a sea of thick fur, and when the tide bore me away and (note this) I was willing to be borne off, you came into the water and saved me from drowning. Why? Then, the next night, when I ask you for a little warmth, the least glance of love, you turn your back on me.

O: You must be sick to your mind, or else you are trying to imitate the sphinx cheaply.

L: I dream too much, over and over. I wander far from home and am unable to find the way back through farmland and empty barns . . . Always lost, alien people, immense mountainscapes, in which I wander, seeking.

Roses, narcissi, eucalyptus, mandarin oranges, anemones.

O: (*to change the painful subject away from himself*) Who shall be scapegoat?

A: The weakest member of the cast.

J: Must find the rotting link in this chain.

EDICT MAKER: 295620, the nameless one. A number is more easily erased than a patronymic.

Z: The lights! Out with the lights!

(*The stage lights become unbearably bright. Z covers his eyes with his palms, falls on his hands, and 'walks' on them as if looking for a hole in which to hide himself. A boy brings on two wooden blocks which have leather straps across. He gives them to Z, who fits them onto his hands. As Z walks on them, they sound hollow. With one leg raised and the other hopping, body arched to suggest deformity, Z is acting out a memory of a vagrant begging in the courtyard of a church as the worshippers come out after a* paniyiri.)

Z: (*shouting*) Alms! Alms! (*Shaking his arms*) The celebration of a new saint's day, a festival instituted, a procession must be good for alms. Look! I am an animal performing for your beanfeast. Am I not an entertainment? Close the shops, make carnival, let me dance, invent music, sing songs, visit the shadow theatre, the open-air cinema. The lights! Out with the lights! I filled the chimney with sacks; the Devil still managed to get down. I lit a fire of old cartons; he leaped the flame. He lives on the roof, he looks in at the window. Cover the glass with blankets! He scratches the panes. He tries the door handles. I nailed the doors. If there's a light, he can get in through chinks in the wall.

J: It stands to reason.

EDICT MAKER: The most vulnerable has to be made scapegoat for maximum effect.

J: No half-measures – who coined 'the whole hog'?

A: Everyone with the exception of Z seems to be a little sad – why?

O: Cage life doesn't suit me.

J: Let's play a game.

O: What game?

J: Any. I'll start. WOMAN.

EDICT MAKER: MAN.

A: NIGHT.

O: LIFE.

L: BREAKFAST.

J: GARDEN.

L: FATHER.

A: BAR.

O: WORLD.

A: WAR.

H: Crap! What would you like to experience again before you die?

A: The sight of a flock of sheep, thousands of ewes and lambs pouring down the mountainside at a big gathering, crying the rivers to silence.

H: Are you naïve enough to think that might win you a reprieve?

A: No, not for a moment. Being a polite man, I was simply answering your question.

H: (*bowing*) And I was testing your reflexes.

O: ENGINE.

A: SUN.

J: AEGEAN.

L: SPRING.

O: POOR.

A: AUNT.

EDICT MAKER: GLASS.

GUARD: EYE.

J: Wonderful! If there were a sky to stare at, to stare blindly at the sky.

GUARD: (*to* H) You are a person without will power.

O: I want a glass of water.

H: Never before did I have the power of life and death, and I find myself impotent.

GUARD: So, you consider blowing out your own brains?

H: I must have revenge.

GUARD: For what?

H: For having been betrayed into being born.

GUARD: Are you planning to use the gun on yourself?

A: It happened to a man I knew. His brains tumbled out, hot and steaming onto the grass.

H: Aah! (*He runs into the corridor, is heard vomiting. The prisoners look at the whip. He returns, wiping his mouth.*) They say you feel better, once you've vomited. I feel worse.

J: Let's make an agreement.

O: Yes, compromise is the only solution.

J: You say you are lonely out there. Why not have one of us be your aide-de-camp, to carry messages, contact headquarters, tidy your desk, arrange excursions to the beach?

H: If I thought one of you could be trusted – why are you laughing? – I'd entertain the idea.

J: Shut your eyes and let God direct your hand.

H: Stop joking.

J: Don't say anything. Simply shut your eyes and point a finger towards one of us.

H: (*obeys, but his forefinger wavers in the air, stopping at the extreme right – cage number 6, which is of course empty*) There, you shall be my lieutenant. Who are you? (*Opening his eyes*) Oh, nobody.

J: Try again. Shut your eyes, turn round twice, and point.

EDICT MAKER: The other day –

O: Be quiet.

A: (*to* L) I'll take you to Italy.

H: That one – who is it?

O: He's picked Z: an inspired choice.

Z: (*shouting*) Don't hurt me. My physician won't allow it. Look, I'll swallow the angels – they'll protect me.

EDICT MAKER: Do as you please. I'm beginning to believe in your devils. We are too much alike for comfort at close quarters.

H: Don't get frightened. I'll be your friend and make you head of Intelligence or Administration. How would you like to be night watchman? (*Unlocking the gate of cage 1, pulling Z out quickly, while keeping the gun trained on the* EDICT MAKER, *then waving the revolver in the air*) There's no need to be afraid. Look! I have the gun.

Z: What a charming person. Such a friendly gesture.

(*Z waves his arms in imitation of* H, *pointing his forefinger to represent the revolver. A pistol shot corresponds with his movement.*)

H: (*severely*) You should never play with firearms. Many boys have orphaned themselves in that way.

Z: O Sir, yes Sir! I'll be careful in future. I've a gun, I've a gun!

(*He again goes through the motions of firing a revolver. Nothing happens. In a panic, he fires again and again.*)

H: (*in a mild voice*) You've probably run out of ammunition.

Z: Lend me yours, Sir?

H: No. Never lend your wife your harp or your gun –

A: Dad used to say.

H: (*drily*) Dad said a lot of things.

(*J comes quietly to the bars of his cage, while H is musing briefly on the subject of his parent. Catching Z's vacant eye, J points discreetly to the whip that lies between the two men, hoping to make him through dumbshow understand that he should pick it up and use it against H, to strike the revolver from his hand. A gleam comes into Z's eyes, as he realises he can at last have a real weapon against his enemies. He leaps for the whip and cracks it extravagantly about the feet of H.*)

Z: Aha! Aha! (*Strikes the revolver from H's hand*) Down, Lucifer!

H: (*to J*) The comedy's over, if this is your idea of fun. (H *backs towards the cages, his reactions quicker than those of his adversary. It is the first time he has turned his back on the other 'animals'. To J he speaks with fury as he throws him the keys.*) This is where your game ends, you fool. You got me into it, now get me out. If the tablecloth is to be turned, it has to be now.

(*During this time, Z is dancing hysterically about the stage, cracking his new toy, throwing out his legs as if about to break into a Cossack dance.*)

Z: Cut off his tail, see it hiss, see it fry, see it fly.

(*J quickly unlocks his own cage from inside, but once out, hesitates about the others. He then runs to cage 1, releases the* EDICT MAKER, *then to the* GUARD *in cage 3, then L and A in cage 5. Lastly he lets out O from cage 2. O is let out last, for his need is greatest. Each one is intent on laying hands on the fallen gun, but Z constantly lashes over it with the whip.)*

J: It's the humane thing to do, restrain him for his own good.

GUARD: Bring a straitjacket.

(The EDICT MAKER goes for one.)

O: Close in, carefully, closer.

Z: Close in, carefully, closer.

O: Don't let him get near the lights.

Z: Don't let him get near the lights.

H: Watch for the Devil's side.

Z: Aaaaaahhhh.

H: What did I tell you? His teeth are probably rotting, to judge by the smell of his breath.

(Shielding his eyes, O deliberately throws himself into the track of the whip, and is successful in getting the thong round his body, which he twists towards Z.)

H: This is your chance. Get him now.

(General fight, in which Z is finally overcome. He has to be held down.)

Z: *Kyrie, eleison.*

O: *Kyrie, eleison*

Z: *Kyrie, eleison.*

O: *Christe, eleison.*

Z: *Christe, eleison.*

O: *Christe, eleison.*

Z: *Kyrie, eleison.*

O: *Kyrie, eleison.*

Z: *Kyrie, eleison.*

Gloria in excelsis Deo, et in terra pax hominibus bonae voluntatis.

(*Loudspeaker, Z's voice.*)

Documents proving have been seized by from the offices of subversive citizens living in northern countries factory hands and semi-students created an organisation of youth in 49 occidental towns in 9 villages affiliated membership activities numberless personalities labour systematically among the workers tactics publish a news-sheet.

EDICT MAKER: (*from the wings, bawling at the top of his voice*) Bar the exits! Bar all exits!

L: Don't let it shock you! I beg of you, keep your seats until order can be restored.

GUARD: Isn't there one among you who has duplicate keys to the outer gates?

L: (*going apart, with lowered head*) I can't bear . . . Why don't I die? Stand by us, merciful God.

Z: As a deer for running water . . .

GUARD: The Edict Maker's been a long time. Why is he taking so long?

O: Look at his eyes, how they flash with green and blue fire.

A: His knees are trembling.

L: He's been on hunger strike too long.

GUARD: It's soup he needs, a good bean soup.

O: What a long way we've come since A said of him: 'He's going to spew the beans.' The bag's burst. Out flow the beans.

(*The* EDICT MAKER *returns, dragging a stretcher-cum-straitjacket.*)

EDICT MAKER: Tickets! Passports! Visas!

A: At this time of night? Here? Now?

EDICT MAKER: We arrive constantly at new frontiers, where it is essential to check credentials. It never seems to have dawned on you that – do you realize the danger we are in? We are never very far ahead of the enemy advance. Does no one here have a sense of reality?

A: I'm going to laugh. It's been growing in me like a cyst – I'll burst, if I don't laugh.

(*He falls down in convulsions of mirth, laughter which turns into untidy sobbing.*)

EDICT MAKER: Passports! Visas! Tickets!

Z: You took my papers, damn you!

(*Breaking away from the other prisoners, Z begins a manic dance which they are too controlled by to interrupt. When he begins to show fatigue, owing to his emaciated condition, they begin to pull themselves together. They fall upon him and restrain his limbs; his jerking head and body they cannot restrain. Suddenly O, H, L, and*

A *begin to weep where they stand, holding the madman.*)

A: What makes you laugh?

EDICT MAKER: These papers are out of date. An entirely new system of identification was instituted yesterday.

O: My arms are tired. If you don't tie him up soon, he'll escape, and run amok through the entire building.

EDICT MAKER: Very well, we'll see to the tickets afterwards. Bring the stretcher.

(*Z is strapped down into the straitjacket in the centre of the stage. L addresses the auditorium.*)

L: Don't let it shock you: they will not harm the imbecile.

Z: Let me out, cowardly swine!

EDICT MAKER: It's a mere formality.

Z: I am Z, son of Z.

EDICT MAKER: (*bending down to pick up the forgotten firearm*) Kill now! Bring them to trial afterwards.

J: Glory after death! Don't miss next week's killings. Have your head blown off by public subscription.

(*The* EDICT MAKER *points the gun wildly among the prisoners, pressing the trigger. Nothing happens. At the same time, synchronised with his feverish pressing of the trigger, a discreet telephone is heard ringing softly but insistently nearby. When the* EDICT MAKER *gives up trying to fire the gun, the telephone too is silent.*)

EDICT MAKER: Don't panic! O'clock, what is it? Noon has set, morning star over the prison-yard says it's antemeridian in October same year next year today never last night dawn has come.

L: Give me back my men, the one I lost, the ones I could have loved.

O: Posthumous laurels! Vine leaves! Immortality to –

ALL: VIVE LES RATS!

O: Water!

EDICT MAKER: To stampede now will cost the lives of innocent bystanders.

J: Are we to be left to die?

(*The eight come together, beseeching help from the audience. Except for cage 6, the cells of the prisoners are brightly lit. The prisoners themselves make a dark mass in the middle of the stage. A young man appears, standing close to the right wings. With raised arms and interlaced fingers, he begins to control a shadow show. Apart from the slight movement of his hands, he is static in a formal ballet position into which he eases himself with a dancer's deliberation.*

A monstrous shadow of a swarm of rats moves from right to left, covering the cages. It is being projected with the rapt ritual of the child's 'rabbit on the wall'.

The rats themselves move across the stage from both sides, flow together into one stream at the head of the steps leading down to the auditorium. Squealing, pattering, rustling, they swarm through the theatre, giving the impression that they are everywhere among the audience.)

O: My throat chokes on grey hair, the world is full of hair, full of sharp teeth. Long tails float on the surface of the flood. A sea of pointed snouts, of grey hair.

YOU HAVE BEEN WARNED: THE RATS ARE DETERMINED TO SURVIVE.

(*Loudspeaker, O's voice.*)

A DISCIPLINED FREEDOM NEVER SUCH FREEDOM THE PEOPLE ARE DELIGHTED A DELIGHTED PEOPLE.

EDICT MAKER: Kill now! Will be shot on sight!

Z: My forebears, Z.

J: Glory after death!

A: Like swine.

O: Water!

(*This is the end of the performance, but as the audience leaves the auditorium, they should be followed by the words* DETERMINED TO SURVIVE, *repeated many times.*)

CONCLUSION

There's your bone, I hope it's dry enough for your taste. The dog buried it months ago. It was bound to be dug up again. Remember us, some of you, when you get home. Light a candle in the window, for the death in all of us.

The following abbreviations are used in these notes:

BC   Brenda Chamberlain

NLW   National Library of Wales

PD   Brenda Chamberlain, *Poems with Drawings* (London: Enitharmon, 1969).

Prot 1   National Library of Wales MS 21491D: first draft of *The Protagonists*.

Prot 2   National Library of Wales, MS 21492D: second draft of *The Protagonists*.

Prot 3   National Library of Wales, MS 21493D: third draft of *The Protagonists*.

Prot 4   National Library of Wales, MS 21494E: acting script of *The Protagonists*.

Prot 5   Gwynedd Archives and Museums Service, Caernarfon Record Office; North Wales Arts Association Archive, XD90/3/11 Brenda Chamberlain: acting script.

Prot 6   National Library of Wales, ex 2735: annotated acting script belonging to Alan ('Phredd') McPherson, who played the Guard. See Figure 12, p. lxxvi.

*

Before the action commences **(p. 6)**: Occupying the place of these initial stage directions in *Prot* 6 (pp. 3–4) is a 'document' that amounts to a political profile – the authorities' secret dramatis personae – of the characters Z, A, J, L and O (H, who is brought on stage later in the play, is not included). The text is for the most part already present in *Prot* 2, the second draft of the play; it is not present in *Prot* 5. The document is headed 'from THE BLACK DOSSIER'; this is clearly the file the Edict Maker will ask the Guard to fetch (together with a branding iron): see pp. 33–4. It is unclear what dramatic use was made of the document in the performance itself; given the fact that Alan McPherson (who played the Guard) has noted 'MOVE FRONT' against O's lines below, it was most likely spoken. Text marked in *Prot* 6 as deleted in performance is identified in square brackets below.

> **Z:** Possibly, the son of L. An hysteric, a fake religious. His papers were not in order. Known to be in contact with revolutionary organisations abroad. Most devious character: to be guarded carefully.
>
> **A:** As a minor civil servant[,] could not on demand produce a satisfactorily clean sheet of his political activities over the past twenty years. Formerly as a student of our celebrated university, and more recently as a lecturer at this same seat of learning, he indulged his inflammatory interests. [As a student he has hidden for some months in the mountains[;] eventually captured on the way to visit his parents, he was imprisoned with six other men and a prostitute. History repeats itself.]
> At the time of his new arrest, he spoke wildly, as if having taken leave of his senses, about love of his land and fellow countrymen.
>
> **J:** Had recently written 50 poems of a subversive nature which, printed on an underground press, have been circulated among seamen, dockers, and shipwrights in many seaports.
>
> **L:** May be the mother of Z; on the other hand, she may not. A farm woman, whether wife, widow, or

unmarried mother, is not certainly known. Could equally be a prostitute or a woman of virtue. [Suspected of having given shelter to enemies of the state, it is more than likely that she was acting as liaison to certain wanted persons in cooperation with rebels in the north. Arrested whilst walking through the old Turkish quarter, leading a convoy laden with panniers of grapes. Under the fruit, in one basket, were seditious pamphlets.]

O: A quiet man, an introvert, of good family. Studying languages at the University. Arrested whilst delivering a lecture on so-called 'intellectual freedom'.

At the very end of the play (p. 72), the eight protagonists are joined by a 'young man' who controls a 'shadow show'; in the earliest draft, *Prot* 1, this figure is described as 'a boy'(p. 3). The list of dramatis personae in *Prot* 2 states of O: 'to be watched – he claims to have weak sight'; and of Z: 'self-conscious image of the holy man' (p. 6). *Prot* 3 identifies A as a 'middle-aged man', O as a 'young man', Z as an 'old-young man', and H simply as 'another prisoner' (p. 3). In the same text, BC's annotation identifies J as a 'poet artist', H as a 'conformist', and Z as 'religious', by which she may mean 'a religious' – i.e. a priest (p. 46).

PRO … THE AGONISTS (p. 3): As a kind of epitaphic subtitle, BC fractures the word 'Protagonists' until its classical Greek etymology is laid bare. An 'agonist' is literally 'a combatant in the games', and by extension, 'a person engaged in a contest or struggle' (*OED*). At the foot of the title-page in *Prot* 5 is 'Brenda Chamberlain / Ydra 1967 / October–November'; *Prot* 2 carries BC's Bangor address at the time – '10 Menai View / Upper Bangor / Caerns, N. Wales'.

As the woman . . . shock you (p. 5): Not present in *Prot* 6 (in which this Preface appears in Alan McPherson's own hand). Annotation in *Prot* 6 indicates that in performance, this preface was spoken by the Guard. In *Prot* 5, the Preface is dated 'Ydra, October–November 1967'.

Give me a dry bone . . . melancholy (p. 5): Included in *PD*, p. 26 (with 'pine' excised), opposite a 'collage' drawing (dated 'October 1966') of quadrilateral and circular forms against a grid-like background.

For winter . . . better time (p. 5): The handwritten Preface in *Prot* 6 rationalises this to: 'For summer a Turkish room / for spring love / autumn melancholy / Winter – a looking forward to a better time'.

Why can't now be good? (p. 5): Following this in *Prot* 6: 'Music'.

***The men stand with their legs . . . the width of their new world* (pp. 6–7)**: In *Prot* 2 and *Prot* 3, BC includes drawings of the prisoners' positions at various points in the play. For her representation of the prisoners' physical appraisal of the 'new world' of their cells, see Figure 13, p. 4 (from *Prot* 3, p. 11).

The men who are in power . . . likenesses (p. 8): BC quotes these opening lines in an interview with William Tydeman (then a lecturer in the Department of English, University College of North Wales, Bangor), broadcast on BBC Radio 4 Wales on 4 April 1968 as part of the monthly arts programme, *Spectrum*. She explained that having experienced a six-month creative impasse following the coup, she found herself 'putting down statements' from which *The Protagonists* developed.

a certain rock (p. 8): The island setting is based on the internment island of Léros in the Dodecanese, close to the Turkish coast, to which the Greek military junta exiled political undesirables after the coup of April 1967. In her BBC Radio 4

Wales *Spectrum* interview, broadcast on 4 April 1968, BC states that she visited Léros twice, in May and August 1967.

The rats . . . rodent ship (p. 8): *Prot* 1 has the subtitle 'THE RODENT SHIP'. *Prot* 2 is subtitled 'WORD OUT OF LEROS'. Written on Ídhra, NLW MS 21500E is BC's journal for 1966, entitled 'A Total Eclipse of the Sun'. The entry for 30 July (p. 57) runs: 'We should be transformed into lemmings, run down into the sea, and swim until we die of swimming'. The entry for 27 August reads: 'Shall I tell you the truth of how desperate we are? My old friend ＿＿＿＿ [name not given] is hunting for yet another house to rent. The last one is too dirty and rat-infested' (p. 58).

This creature . . . narrow teeth (p. 8): Included in *PD*, p. 13 (with 'secret' excised), opposite an image of a hairy, creaturely form, dated 1965.

The EDICT MAKER . . . *followed by the* GUARD (p. 8): On the evidence of *Prot* 6, the Edict Maker and the Guard came on stage after O's line: 'It stinks' (p. 9). *Prot* 6 also suggests that they entered onto the scaffolding above the prisoners' cages, and that the prisoners could be locked in their cages by the Guard from above. In *Prot* 4, BC notes: 'Throughout the play, each official entrance of the Edict Maker and every loud-speaker edict is preceded by a recognisable clarion call. The fruit eaten by the Guard during the course of the play are apples, which he peels with a sheath knife kept in his belt. He may also use it to clean his nails' (p. 1). The notes on the performance copy of *The Protagonists* used by the stage manager, Joy Ostle (Joy Roberts in 1968), refer to a 'pulpit' – probably an old lectern – placed stage right, from which some of the Edict Maker's pronouncements were delivered.

The garbageman . . . straight ahead (p. 9): On the evidence of *Prot* 6, deleted in performance.

NO BEATNIKS ... SHORES (p. 9): Cf. BC's poem, 'Nisi Leros' ('Léros Island'), published in *Poetry Wales* 5, 3 (Spring 1970), p. 12: 'No beatniks, odd-bodies, or starving poets / are allowed on these shores, it is the time of // the great barbola and tea-shop society; / only artists with easels are acceptable // At the madhouse, grey sheets dry fast / in the killing sun. On the site of Lerian // Artemis, political prisoners envy the snails'.

WILL BE SHOT ON SIGHT (p. 9): Cf. BC's 1968 *Forecast* interview with Alan McPherson (Appendix 3, p. 117 below): 'And everybody just listening to the hourly bulletins – it was totally negative. You see, everything was, "If you do this, SHOT ON SIGHT." "If you do that you'll be SHOT ON SIGHT"'.

STIN IGIA SAS (p. 9): A transliteration of the Greek 'Στην υγειά σας': 'To your health'. Annotation at this point in *Prot* 6 (for the Guard): 'down [from the upper scaffolding] to start recitation'.

Can it be proved ... men rats (p. 10): On the evidence of *Prot* 6, excised in performance.

If circling outwards ... difficult to imagine (p. 10): A dense passage. 'A Total Eclipse of the Sun' – the title of BC's 1966 Ídhra journal – reveals the experience to have been BC's own: '"They" won't leave me alone anywhere, not even in the monasteri [*sic*]. I only want to light a candle in the church but the sacristan comes, thinking I have not put money in the brass offertory box. Next he asks, all hopeless-hopeful, have I a cigarette. He has a crumpled face, like a sodden cigarette stub. Once, he presented me with a gardenia from an offering of flowers under an ikon of the virgin' (NLW MS 21500E, pp. 57–8; entry for 27 August 1966).

Among the fat bodies ... sign (p. 10): Annotation in *Prot* 6: 'expansively'.

The dead whisper . . . second time (p. 10): Cast as two three-line stanzas in *PD*, pp. 8-9, underneath a long graph-like background extending across two pages on which there are numerous rock forms (dated September 1966). The lines were also included in BC's Welsh Arts Council 'Word and Image' exhibition of 1970.

The **EDICT MAKER** *walks off . . . with their eyes* **(p. 10):** On the evidence of *Prot* 6, excised in performance. It is clear from *Prot* 6 that the actual entrances and exits of the Guard and the Edict Maker differed from those indicated in the playscript.

Out there among the leaves . . . reputations (p. 10): BC summoned this image of the police as locusts in her BBC Radio 4 Wales *Spectrum* interview of 4 April 1968. The image is the central metaphor of a brief poem, 'Concentration Camp', that appears in three drafts in NLW MS 21485E, pp. 154–6. The poem follows two drafts of a poem, dated winter 1969, entitled 'Military Policeman': 'A HEAD AS BIG AS A SAUCEPAN! // FILLED WITH BONES AND WATER, / IT WOULD FEED MANY PEASANTS' (pp. 152–3).

The lips of the sea . . . allowed to know (p. 11): Included in *PD*, p. 20 as the first two verse paragraphs of a poem (completed by lines from the next formal chorus of the play, beginning 'Where does that road go?') opposite an aggregation of pebbles and rocks against a grey background covered with gridlines; within the same frame is an image of Welsh mountains or hills in cross-section. The image is dated 'August 1966 YΔPA [Ydra/Ídhra]'. The poem was also included in BC's Welsh Arts Council 'Word and Image' exhibition of 1970.

The moon has fallen down . . . never be allowed to know (p. 11): A direct recollection of BC's two trips to the internment island of Léros in the Dodecanese. As BC explained in her 1968 *Forecast* interview (Appendix 3, p. 118 below): 'that part at the beginning [of *The Protagonists*] when someone says, "the mountains whose geography we shall never be allowed to know" – well, this came from various views of the marvellous mountains, actually on the next island, but it looked as though it was part of the same island. To me it was like a prison, the whole island – I began to feel like a prisoner, too'.

***Prisoners retreat . . . chains* (p. 11)**: Annotation in *Prot* 6: 'exit – turn lights out'.

Yes, they go out . . . sullen (p. 12): Annotation in *Prot* 6: 'Hawk up'. Cf. the entry under 12 March in BC's Ídhra journal for 1966, 'A Total Eclipse of the Sun' (NLW MS 21500E, p. 44): 'Orange blossom is out. After storm, almonds litter the yard outside the garden door. The weather comes and goes, blowing now hot[,] now cold, calm, tempest, sullen, smiling'.

So was I . . . a little water (p. 13): O's repeated requests for water activates the ironic pun in his name: O/'eau'.

Your type always asks for water (p. 13): Annotation in *Prot* 6: 'SPIT'.

It has happened . . . to be able to die (pp. 13–14): BC's annotation in *Prot* 1, p. 4: 'take very fast'. In the same typescript (p. 28), these lines are followed by a modern Greek translation.

I was born / to have . . . to be able to die (p. 14): The lines appear (with three small changes of order) in *PD*, p. 1, opposite a simple drawing whose contours suggest a sheer cliff-face, seen side-on. The image is dated 'June 1961'.

I was born / to begin . . . to take (p. 14): Annotation in *Prot* 6 indicates that the Guard cracked his whip after these lines were delivered, and that the prisoners knelt. It is unclear whether the Guard was on stage or in the wings at this point.

I was born . . . to be able to die (p. 14): Perhaps surprisingly for such a resonant line, this is marked as excised in *Prot* 6. BC's epitaph in Glanadda Cemetery, Bangor runs: 'BRENDA CHAMBERLAIN / 11 July 1971 / Artist, Writer, Poet / "I was born to live / I was born to die"'.

I need water . . . to the west (pp. 14–15): BC's annotation in *Prot* 1, p. 4: 'take very fast'.

Where does that road go . . . And fresh water (pp. 14–15): With small changes, and excising 'Only a fool leaves oars in a boat' and 'Blessings on the head of that man, whoever he may be', the lines appear in *PD*, p. 20 as verse paragraphs 3–6 of the poem beginning 'The lips of the sea'. (For the first two verse paragraphs, and BC's corresponding graphic image, see the note on 'The lips of the sea', p. 81 above). The aggregate poem was included in BC's Welsh Arts Council 'Word and Image' exhibition of 1970.

We'd need a lot of luck . . . sea level (p. 15): On the evidence of *Prot* 6, delivered with the words 'either on the beach or just as we were pushing out the boat' excised.

GUARD *comes in* **(p. 16)**: Annotation in *Prot* 6 at this point: 'SIT' and 'SMOKE'.

VIVE LA MORT! (p. 16): 'Long live Death!'

What a performance! . . . going where? (p. 16): Cf. an entry for January 1966 (date between 19th and 23rd) in BC's Ídhra journal for 1966, 'A Total Eclipse of the Sun' (NLW MS 21500E, p. 33), perhaps with an ironic echo of Matthew 8:30 – 'The foxes have holes, and the birds of the air have nests; but the Son of man hath not where to lay his head': 'The foreigners have houses, and yet they sit huddled together in the draughts and noise of Tasso's Taverna, hysterically unable to lead private lives at home; keeping stiff upper lips, braced against the horrible Greeks, bearing up like refugees, being ugly together. Why do they come here? "Trapped[,]" as the American girl said to me, "O God, for New York." The sick getting sicker, on the way to the unmysterious East'. The January and February sections of the journal were published posthumously as 'A Total Eclipse of the Sun' in *Mabon* (Spring 1972), pp. 6–13; the section quoted here appears on p. 8.

Is this a gathering . . . you are guilty (p. 17): Annotation in *Prot* 6 suggests that at this point the Guard was consulting a 'Rule Book'.

Can't somebody find . . . ancestry? (p. 17): Marked in *Prot* 6 as delivered after L's lines ending 'into the desert', two lines previously.

To keep sane . . . invent our own lives (p. 18): Cf. the end of BC's *A Rope of Vines: Journal from a Greek Island* (1965), p. 160: 'We invent our own lives, but there remains reality outside oneself, and these enduring boats, laden with melons and water pots, green peppers, and cattle, point the way to life through abundant dying'.

What relief to lie down . . . dog days (p. 18): Cf. the entry for 21 July in BC's Ídhra journal for 1966, 'A Total Eclipse of the Sun' (NLW MS 21500E, p. 55): '"Get to the edge of the bed: for Christ's sake, let me sleep. Our bodies' sweat has stained the burning sheet"'.

Is the last of summer . . . the watershed? (p. 18): Cf. the entry for 28 March in BC's Ídhra journal for 1966, 'A Total Eclipse of the Sun' (NLW MS 21500E, p. 44): 'At last, thanks to God, I am over the watershed of Spring'.

Yesterday, the vine stock . . . tendrils (p. 18): Taken from the entry for 16 April in BC's 1966 Ídhra journal, 'A Total Eclipse of the Sun' (NLW MS 21500E, p. 47).

Love and embrace . . . behind bars (p. 19): In the second half of 1968, at the suggestion of BC's friend Alan Clodd (founder of Enitharmon Press), the Daedalus Press published these lines in the form of one of their attractive 6 x 4 inch 'Poemcards' or 'Pin-up Poems' (Number 11), minus 'Lemon, venetian vetches; orchis, fritillary'. The illustrator Juliet Standing was involved in the project. The card features an attractively simple, fluid line drawing that is unmistakably by BC; see NLW MS 23881D/35, 36. The lines were also included in *PD*, p. 24 (again, minus 'Lemon, venetian vetches . . .') opposite a large graticule on which appear rock and island forms (dated 1968). Cf. the entry for 12 March in BC's Ídhra journal for 1966, 'A Total Eclipse of the Sun' (NLW MS 21500E, p. 43): 'I can love and love (again, I can) with south wind of springtime, south wind of love, almonds fresh to the taste and touch, uncompliant children, smell of clean washing from the line, orchis and fritillary from the mountain slope, vin rosé of Nemea. I can love and love when I know myself loved and remembered. If only I could take hold of the sunset and put it in a letter'.

Lemon, venetian vetches; orchis, fritillary (p. 19): In *Prot* 5, the line is punctuated: 'Lemon, venetian vetches, orchis fritillary'. The present punctuation has been adopted since the line derives from an entry under 12 March in BC's Ídhra journal for 1966, 'A Total Eclipse of the Sun' (NLW MS 21500E, p. 43), from which it is clear that 'lemon' and 'venetian' (a shade darker than scarlet) are adjectives of colour applying to 'vetches', and that BC recognises 'orchis' and 'fritillary' as distinct genera of flowers (as is indeed the case botanically): 'Flowers . . . exotic varieties I only knew before as colour plates in books of flora, rarities that on Ydra grow almost like daisies, different species of orchis, and the miniscule fritillary that is said to grow only on this island, nowhere else in the whole of Greece. There are deep purple vetches glowing out of the yellow-blooming gorse, palest lemon vetches, ven[e]tian red vetches, and other flowers so exquisite[,] small, fragile, one can scarcely believe they have power to break earth so stubborn'.

God on the right side, the Devil on the other (p. 20): Z is modelled on Berthold (Bert) Panĕk, a displaced Pole who had come to Britain after the War. He sought a life of prayer on Bardsey Island in 1956 as the 'caretaker' of a dwelling – Plas Bach – rented by A. H. Armstrong, Gladstone Professor of Greek at Liverpool University, and his wife. Panĕk features as 'Wolfgang' in BC's *Tide-race* (1962). At the end of the first week of January 1959, convinced he was locked in 'mortal combat' with devils, Panĕk suffered a nervous breakdown and had to be taken off the island. The incident was reported in *The Times* ('Pole Taken Off Welsh Island', 8 January 1959, p. 4). For the schizophrenic Panĕk, divided between God and the Devil, see *Tide-race*, pp. 203–10, in particular p. 209: 'Jacob told us afterwards at breakfast that never before had he seen such a phenomenon; one whole side of Wolfgang's body was given over to the Devil, the other side to God. One side of his face was evil and twitching; the other side was smooth and placid . . . He had stroked himself on the "God side"; attacked anyone who approached the "Devil side"'.

There's been an accident . . . leave a message (p. 20): The lines were included in BC's Welsh Arts Council 'Word and Image' exhibition of 1970.

GUARD: Sir (p. 21): Annotation in *Prot* 6 after the Guard's reply: 'Go up top + H'. 'Up top' signifies the level of scaffolding above the prisoners' cages.

Get inside, you bastard (p. 21): Annotation in *Prot* 6: 'Shove the fucker in'.

Blood! Blood! . . . Give me a gun, you there! (p. 22): Annotation in *Prot* 6: 'Guard comes down' – i.e. from the scaffolding above the prisoners' cages.

The things I have seen . . . Give me a gun, you there! (p. 22): Cf. the account in BC's *Tide-race* of the schizophrenic breakdown of the Polish 'hermit', Berthold ('Bert') Panĕk, on Bardsey Island in early January 1959: 'Turning to me and gripping me tightly, he moaned hoarsely: "Give me a gun; give me a gun" . . . Shivering, he muttered, "You don't know what I have seen . . . such things"' (pp. 207, 208). Harold Taylor ('Merfyn Edwards' in BC's *Tide-race*), one of the lighthouse keepers on Bardsey from 1958 to 1961, confirms that BC witnessed Panĕk's panicked appeal for a gun: 'It was a very eerie walk to Plas Bach [Panĕk's dwelling] and Bert was so in terror that he demanded that we sing hymns. Having got him to his place I collected the bowl to return to Brenda, telling him to stay where he was until I got back. Whilst I was at Brenda's with the other two young people, we heard a noise outside, which they later described as being like a bull bellowing, whereupon Bert crashed through the door demanding a gun to kill the Devil. He prostrated himself upon the floor. . . and as he rose grabbed a poker to strike the Devil, which was up the chimney. I took the weapon away from him and decided that the only place he would be safe was back at the lighthouse. We left the premises with the fright-stricken group clutching each other'; 'The Light on Top', *World Lighthouse Society Newsletter*, 8, 3 (2010), p. 12 (*http://www.worldlighthouses.org/WLS%20Newsletter%203rd%20Qtr%202010.pdf*, accessed 21 June 2011). See also the note to 'God on the right side', p. 86 above.

Sir, be careful . . . never be trusted (p. 22): Annotation in *Prot* 6: 'BLOCK O's VIEW OF Z'.

the soldier tickled my throat with our breadknife (p. 22): Cf. the dramatic section in *Tide-race* in which BC describes the 'spiritual chaos' of the Polish 'hermit', Berthold Panĕk, whose mental collapse she experienced on Bardsey Island:

'It may have been a clue to hysteria, to his schizophrenia, the remark he let fall in conversation on his first Christmas here. "A Russian tickled my throat with a knife, ha! ha!"' (p. 210). See also the note to 'God on the right side', p. 86 above.

Justus ut palma florebit . . . in domo Domini (p. 23): An ellipsis of verses 13–14 of Psalm 91 from the Clementine Latin Vulgate, included in the Roman Missal. In the Knox Version (since that is the translation L and J use when they act as Z's interpreters): 'The innocent man will flourish as the palm-tree flourishes; he will grow to greatness as the cedars grow on Lebanon. [Planted in] the temple of the Lord[, growing up in the very courts of our God's house, the innocent will flourish . . .]'. The Pole Berthold Panĕk, whose mental breakdown BC witnessed on Bardsey Island, also uttered 'words garbled at random from the Mass'; see *Tide-race*, pp. 205 and 208, together with the note to 'God on the right side', p. 86 above.

ludens in orbe terrarum; et deliciae meae esse cum filiis hominum (p. 23): Z quotes *Proverbs* 8:31 from the Clementine Latin Vulgate, included in the Roman Missal. L translates him in the next line, using the Knox Version.

mea culpa, mea culpa, mea maxima culpa (p. 23): A formula in the Confiteor ('I confess') prayer from the Mass in the Roman Rite of the Catholic Church. L acts as Z's translator in the next line. Harold Taylor, one of the Bardsey lighthouse keepers during BC's time there, confirms that the lines were uttered by the Pole, Berthold Panĕk, during his mental breakdown: 'In the early evening I went to Will's house to tell him that the ship had agreed to pick up Bert [Panĕk] on the relief. Whilst I was there Bert burst in and demanded that we protect him from the Devil, and wanted the fire put out because the Devil was up the chimney. They were all pretty shaken. More especially because he would continually prostrate himself on the floor, head toward the fire with arms widespread crying "Mea Culpa" three or four times'; 'The Light on Top', *World Lighthouse Society Newsletter*, 8, 3 (2010), p. 12 (*http://www.worldlighthouses.org/WLS%20 Newsletter%203rd%20Qtr%202010.pdf*, accessed 21 June 2011). See also the note to 'God on the right side', p. 86 above.

Quomodo potest homo nasci . . . et renasci? **(p. 25):** Nicodemus's question to Christ; John 3:4. L translates Z in the next line, using the Knox Version.

Why don't you give him soup? (p. 25): In *Tide-race* (p. 206), BC recalls that she prepared a bowl of soup for the Pole, Berthold Panĕk, in the terrible days of early January 1959 during which he suffered a schizophrenic breakdown – a detail confirmed by Harold Taylor, one of the lighthouse-keepers: see 'The Light on Top', *World Lighthouse Society Newsletter*, 8, 3 (2010), p. 12 (*http://www.worldlighthouses.org/WLS%20Newsletter%20 3rd%20Qtr%202010.pdf*, accessed 21 June 2011).

Roman Missal (p. 26): The liturgical book containing the texts and 'rubrics' used in the Roman Catholic Mass.

IN NOMINE PATRIS . . . AMEN **(p. 26)**: The 'trinitarian formula' used in the rites and liturgies of various Christian churches, deriving from Matthew 28:19. It is translated by L in the next line.

et quare tristis incedo . . . inimicus? **(p. 26)**: Psalm 42:2 from the Clementine Latin Vulgate, included in the Roman Missal: '[For thou art God my strength: why hast thou cast me off?] and why do I go sorrowful whilst the enemy afflicteth me?'. L's translation in the next line is based on the Knox Version.

Dirigatur, Domine . . . vespertinum **(p. 26)**: Psalm 140:2 from the Clementine Latin Vulgate, included in the Roman Missal; translated by J this time, in the Knox Version.

I have no merchandise . . . nicknames, nationality, religion (p. 27): A short while before her death in July 1971, BC recorded a poem – 'Why did you ring me?' (preserved in NLW ex 2436) – for the Welsh Arts Council's 'Dial-a-poem' scheme; the poem incorporated an inflection of Z's lines.

eisteddfodau **(p. 27)**: Plural of *eisteddfod*, a Welsh festival of literature, music and drama.

En ipse stat . . . myrrha electa **(p. 27)**: The *Canticum Canticorum* (Song of Songs or Song of Solomon), 2:9, from the Clementine Latin Vulgate; the text is included in the Roman Missal. L translates in the Knox Version.

Sicut balsamum aromatizans . . . myrrha electa **(p. 27)**: Ecclesiasticus 24:20, from the Clementine Latin Vulgate; properly: 'Sicut cinnamomum, et balsamum aromatizans odorem dedi: quasi myrrha electa dedi suavitatem odoris' ('Cinnamon and odorous balm have no scent like mine; the choicest myrrh has no such fragrance'), to which J's translation (Knox Version) adheres.

I am a priest . . . unfrocked! (p. 28): A recollection, perhaps, of the opening of 'The Jungle' by BC's friend and collaborator, Alun Lewis: 'In mole-blue indolence the sun / Plays idly on the stagnant pool / In whose grey bed black swollen leaf / Holds Autumn rotting like an unfrocked priest'. BC would have known that priest's robes were kept at Plas Bach, Bardsey Island, where Z's prototype, Berthold Paněk – the would-be 'hermit' of Bardsey, whose mental collpase she witnessed on the island – lived. As Harold Taylor, one of the Bardsey lighthouse keepers, recalls: 'Again we had to go through the performance of singing hymns as we stumbled along the uneven cart track till we reached his abode, which [Paněk] would not go beyond. I told him I would not leave him up the island as he was frightening everyone there. He finally acceded to accompany me if I would go with him to the house and collect the priest's robes so that the devil would not get them. We entered the house and he showed me where the robes were and started packing them in a suitcase to take with us. I said that we could not do this, as the night was so wet that they would get damaged. It would be best if I locked them in the cupboard and took the key away with us. He agreed to this and we made our way to the lighthouse'; 'The Light on Top', *World Lighthouse Society Newsletter*, 8, 3 (2010), p. 12 *(http://www. worldlighthouses.org/WLS%20Newsletter%203rd%20Qtr%20 2010.pdf*, accessed 21 June 2011). See also the note to 'God on the right side', p. 86 above.

You out there . . . in front of my face (p. 28): Inflected for the poem 'Why did you ring me?', which BC recorded as part of the Welsh Arts Council's 'Dial-a-poem' scheme in 1971: 'Out there, how does it feel? / are there bars in front of your face?'. Phrases from J's next two pronouncements and from L's next speech are also included in the poem.

A garden, never walked through (p. 29): It is clear from *Prot* 6 that at this point, the Guard cynically interrupted J in performance: an added intervention – 'a what?' – is inserted after 'garden'. A further note in *Prot* 6 at this point runs: 'pen + pad of paper', indicating that the Guard is taking notes during these exchanges.

One brown sheep grazed there (p. 29): Another added interruption – 'a what[?]' – is indicated in *Prot* 6 after 'sheep'.

One brown sheep . . . solitary sheep (p. 29): A possible allusion to one of the narratives of formative loss, recollection and insight known as 'Spots of Time' in Wordsworth's *The Prelude*: 'And afterwards the wind and sleety rain, / And all the business of the elements, / The single sheep, and the one blasted tree, / And the bleak music of that old stone wall / . . .

All these were spectacles and sounds to which / I often would repair, and thence would drink / As at a fountain' (1805; XI, 375–84). The 'drinking-trough' that is 'shaped like a small coffin' under a cypress tree may also recall the 'heap of earth' beneath the thorn tree that is 'like an infant's grave in size' in Wordsworth's 'The Thorn' from *Lyrical Ballads*.

caïque (p. 29): 'A light boat or skiff' (*OED*).

The splendour of the moon . . . chocolate-perfumed towns (p. 30): On the evidence of *Prot* 6, excised in performance. The lines were recast as part of a poem – 'Why did you ring me?' – that BC recorded for the Welsh Arts Council's 'Dial-a-poem' scheme in 1971.

Whatever I say . . . in front of a judge (p. 31): Recast as part of 'Why did you ring me?', recorded in 1971 for the Welsh Arts Council's 'Dial-a-poem' scheme.

Look at me, a deluded Samson . . . pillars of your house (p. 31): See Judges 16:29–30.

How long . . . dangerous without his beard (p. 31): On the evidence of *Prot* 6, excised in performance.

Because he sees sparrows as eagles (p. 33): Perhaps an allusion to the tale of the sparrow and the eagle in the *One Thousand and One Nights*. Cf. also *Macbeth*, I, ii, 33–5: 'Dismay'd not this / Our captains, Macbeth and Banquo? Yes, / As sparrows eagles, or the hare the lion'.

Bring the black dossier (p. 33): The totalitarian state's secret profiles; see the first note in this section (p. 75 above).

Samson Z . . . pulled down, not his (p. 33): On the evidence of *Prot* 6, excised in performance.

Was in an easier time . . . happen tomorrow (p. 33): Given to A, J, O and L in *Prot* 6.

What was the General doing? . . . Dictator (pp. 33–4): On the evidence of *Prot* 6, excised in performance.

You are no longer Z, but number 295620 (p. 34): Annotation in *Prot* 6 indicates that this was the end of the first half of the performance. Further annotation in *Prot* 6 reveals how the beginning of the second half was managed: '[Edict Maker] and I [the Guard] enter . . . noises | crack [of whip] – | music starts | 3 prisoners enter | crack | 3 more enter | crack | music stops'.

Such guilt I feel towards women! (p. 34): Cf. the account in BC's *Tide-race* of the spiritual crisis and breakdown of the Polish 'hermit', Berthold Panĕk: 'In those early days, while he was still comparatively normal, he asked whether he might visit us sometimes, for it was not an easy thing for him to do; to cut himself off from wine, women, and song . . . On the last night, in his raving, he contradicted himself at every turn. He would shriek, "A man must live without sex." And again, "I have a wife in Poland." And then, "I am not married"' (p. 210). Harold Taylor, one of the lighthouse keepers on Bardsey from 1958 to 1961, notes: 'It appears that [Panĕk] had some secret guilt from his days in Poland and had tried to enter monasteries all over Europe, especially Italy. He had been rejected as being an unsuitable character. He had ultimately arrived at Downside Abbey [a Benedictine monastery in Somerset], where again he was tested and found unsuitable . . . Bert came from Silesia, a territory claimed by Germany, so he was forced into the army to fight against his own people, and I think this caused his problems'; 'The Light on Top', *World Lighthouse Society Newsletter*, 8, 3 (2010), p. 13 (*http:// www.worldlighthouses.org/WLS%20Newsletter%203rd%20 Qtr%202010.pdf*, accessed 21 June 2011). See also the note to 'God on the right side', p. 86 above.

Vide humilitatem meam (p. **34**): Psalm 24:18 in the Clementine Latin Vulgate, included in the Roman Missal: 'Vide humilitatem meam, et laborem meum: et dimitte universa delicta mea'. In the Knox Version: 'Restless and forlorn, I claim your pity, to my sins be merciful'.

Hide me under your downy armpit (p. 35): Cf. the account in BC's *Tide-race* of the mental collapse of the Polish 'hermit', Berthold Panĕk: 'We tried to quieten him, saying that Paul was away, not on the island at all; but he was beyond comprehension, and whispered to me, "Hide me in the most secret cupboard in the dark; anywhere; under the stairs, away from the devils"' (p. 207). See also the note to 'God on the right side', p. 86 above.

Give me a gun! . . . back into her cage (p. 35): On the evidence of *Prot* 6, excised in performance.

God keep you . . . corpse in a narrow place? (pp. 35–6): On the evidence of *Prot* 6, excised in performance.

Stamboul (p. 35): A common variant form of 'Istanbul' until the 1930s.

corpse in narrow place (p. 36): Cf. the entry for 12 March in BC's Ídhra journal for 1966, 'A Total Eclipse of the Sun' (NLW MS 21500E, p. 44): 'The deathbell tolled at about 10 in the morning. Another dead . . . Coming home up steps I never use, very steep towards Calypso's home, heard a dirge and more than a few footsteps. Bearers were with difficulty bringing down to the port the body of an old woman; black polished shoes, hands tied together, mouth stuffed with cotton wool, grey hair, the solid arms of a working woman. In that place, the stairs are so steep, the possibility of her pitching forward out of the coffin seemed not remote. Is it ill or good luck to meet with a corpse in a narrow place?'.

'Buttoned and stitched and closed'? (p. 38): On the evidence of *Prot* 6, excised in performance. O here is presumably referring to L's lines 'After they had taken him away, I began to lose memory of certain events, was busy with needle and thread sewing buttons on lips, stitching tongue to cheek' (p. 17).

There is never an end . . . the bird on the winter sea (p. 38): Included, with some small inflections, in *PD*, p. 7, opposite one of the freer, lighter images in the book: a rock-form with a double outline, dated July 1966.

We flow like wine . . . out of archaic moulds (p. 38): On the evidence of *Prot* 6, excised in performance.

Paix, amitié, coopération **(p. 38)**: 'Peace, friendship, cooperation.' An ironic slogan.

Le progrès par l'unité et l'amour **(p. 38)**: 'Progress through unity and love.' Again, a motto heavy with irony.

Le progrès par l'unité et l'amour . . . variations **(pp. 38-9)**: On the evidence of *Prot* 6, excised in performance.

(*the record still playing* . . . g l o r i o u s r e v o l u t i o n (p. 39-40): On the evidence of *Prot* 6, excised in performance.

Now I am Dick . . . *Not* subtle (p. 40): Cf. the entry for 2 January in BC's Ídhra journal for 1966, 'A Total Eclipse of the Sun' (NLW MS 21500E, p. 30): 'The foreign colony at Tasso's [Taverna] were this morning being shadowed by a plain-clothes Dick. Pick-up, loaf of bread, newspaper – Not subtle'; and the entry for 3 January 1966: 'The Dick is still watching the marijuana-takers'. These entries appeared posthumously in 'A Total Eclipse of the Sun', *Mabon* (Spring 1972), p. 6.

idles on, in an abstracted mood **(p. 41)**: On the evidence of *Prot* 6, excised in performance.

Why not? (p. 41): On the evidence of *Prot* 6, excised in performance.

For sweet Mary's sake . . . play to end now? (p. 42): Given to A in *Prot* 6.

Tact won't solve anything (p. 42): 'So much play on play' (as O has just claimed) indeed: J's 'tact' punningly abridges O's 'to act'.

Mou aresei na kolympo me to feggari **(p. 42)**: A transliteration of the modern Greek Μου αρέσει να κολυμπώ με το φεγγάρι: 'I like to swim when the moon is shining'.

It's my temperament . . . blind beggars shall not find me (p. 42): Cf. the entry under 31 March in BC's Ídhra journal for 1966, 'A Total Eclipse of the Sun' (NLW MS 21500E, p. 45): 'Beggarwomen sometimes come to the door. They are well-fed, brown, in peasant costume, begging for drachmas. Two men also come. One is blind, whitey-blue[-]eyed. The blind one reaches through the grille, groping for money, while the other whines'; and the entry for 28 April (p. 47): 'A swordfish being dismembered: the sword very long. Dead, no energy, vulnerable, should keep myself within the garden gate, the panes of the door open but the grilles firm, so that the blind beggar's groping hand shall not find me'.

This man strikingly resembles my father (p. 43): Cf. *Macbeth*, II, ii, 12–13: 'Had he not resembled / My father as he slept, I had done't'.

'Clawmarks of small birds in black sand' (p. 44): In quotation marks in *Prot* 5, perhaps metadramatically to denote a quotation from BC's own observations on Léros. The bay at Gourna, on the east side of the island, is famous for its black and dark green sand.

Sir, you are putting words into my mouth (p. 44): Annotation in *Prot* 6: 'Wait for A O J to point at me'.

Do I seem nervous, Sir? . . . down there (p. 44): Annotation in *Prot* 6: 'Wait for A O J'. Cf. previous note.

GUARD: Sir (p. 44): Annotation in *Prot* 6: 'Wait for A O J'. Cf. previous two notes.

The boat is there . . . fishing line and bait (p. 44): Annotation in *Prot* 6: 'Kneel etc' (referring to the Guard).

I could, I should have . . . strong in my ears (p. 45): Cf. the lines that appear as a kind of epigraph to BC's Ídhra journal for 1966, 'A Total Eclipse of the Sun' (NLW MS 21500E, p. 29): 'I could, I should destroy myself, from the roof into the almond tree, on the black night wind while the drum still beats to overlay the sound of my fall'. The lines appeared posthumously in 'A Total Eclipse of the Sun', *Mabon* (Spring 1972), p. 6.

You can take pride . . . being in the right (p. 45): Annotation in *Prot* 6: 'SLOWLY' and 'Cross stage on knees and sit on edge of stage[;] eat me [*sic*] buns'.

LA POLITIQUE ÉTRANGÈRE . . . ALLIANCES (p. 46): Literally: 'The government's foreign policy remains unchanged from the form in which it was set out from the first days of the revolution. Good good relations with all states without regard to differences in their social and political system and it definitely remains faithful faithful faithful faithful in its alliances'.

TELLE QUE TRACÉE . . . ALLIANCES (p. 46): On the evidence of *Prot* 6, excised in performance.

WE SEE ALL AROUND . . . LABEUR INTENSE (p. 46): On the evidence of *Prot* 6, deleted in performance.

UN ACCUEIL SPONTANÉ . . . LA FOI HEUREUSE (pp. 46–7): 'A spontaneous and warm welcome / The fruits of intense labour. / Down with the ruins! Down with the Ruins! / United united united / Loving each other / Let us enter the arena / In order to emerge / Victorious victorious victorious / Anew / Our faith proud / Our faith happy.'

ET NOUS AIMANT . . . LA FOI HEUREUSE (p. 47): On the evidence of *Prot* 6, excised in performance.

My thirst has come back! . . . AVEC L'AIDE DE DIEU! (pp. 47–8): On the evidence of *Prot* 6, excised in performance.

GARDIENS VIGILANTS . . . AVEC L'AIDE DE DIEU! (pp. 47–8): 'Vigilant guardians / Of life / Of honour / Of security / Of liberty / Of territorial integrity / Neutralise the enemy! / Neutralise the enemy! / Just as Apollo / As Apollo / At Delphi had killed / The python the python the py– / To create light / With God's help / With God's help.' The classical reference is to the slaying by Apollo (god of light and the sun) of the monstrous serpent-dragon at Delphi and his appropriation of the oracle there. The original mythic name of Delphi was Pytho, from pythein, 'to rot', alluding to the Python's decomposing corpse.

LE PYTHON LE PYTHON LE PY– (p. 48): Cf. BC's 1968 *Forecast* interview with Alan McPherson (Appendix 3, p. 121 below): 'On Sundays they have this thing with loudspeakers in the squares, just battering at the people; one just hears this voice – its indoctrination. At the end of the play the edicts are distorted to make them sound comic, but they are taken from the newspapers: that thing about the python and "castrate the enemy" – that was actually in the Athens news. Sounds mad'.

O there were rats . . . pussy-cats (p. 49): A parodic version of the army/scouting song, 'The Quartermaster's Stores':

'There are rats, rats, rats, big as alley cats / In the store, in the store; / There are / rats, rats, rats, big as alley cats / In the Quartermaster's store'.

Quid igitur lex? **(p. 49)**: Galatians, 3:19 in the Clementine Latin Vulgate, included in the Roman Missal. In the Knox translation: 'What, then, is the purpose of the law?'. Paul's epistle goes on: 'It was brought in to make room for transgression, while we waited for the coming of that posterity, to whom the promise had been made. Its terms were dictated by angels, acting through a spokesman'.

The **GUARD** *goes out briefly . . . carefully* **(p. 49)**: On the evidence of *Prot* 6, excised in performance. Annotation in *Prot* 6 at this point: 'sitting on edge of stage[,] pour out water → mug'.

L *puts her arms through the bars . . . goes out* **(p. 50)**: On the evidence of *Prot* 6, excised in performance. Annotation in *Prot* 6: 'Whip up at her [L]'.

It looks to be . . . I think (p. 50): Annotation in *Prot* 6: 'STAY ON TOP LEVEL'.

our deep sorrow . . . Thursday (p. 50): Alan McPherson recalls that in performance, the Edict Maker, pacing around in shock, reads this letter from his political masters 'partly out loud and partly silently, so that what we hear is nonsensical but clear in the import – he is finished'. In three places I have substituted 'duh' for the 'ed' in *Prot* 5: what BC wishes to convey here is what McPherson recalls as the stunned Edict Maker's 'reversed stutter' at the end of the word 'deprived' ('duh' helpfully gives the actual pronunciation of the past participle, and has the added benefit of communicating the Edict maker's dazed incomprehension). In addition, based on McPherson's recollection of how these lines were played,

I have inserted ellipses to denote the Edict Maker's silent mouthing of parts of the letter. There are echoes in the lines of the repeated 'for reasons unknown' in the stream of 'vociferations' that make up Lucky's speech towards the end of Act 1 of Samuel Beckett's *Waiting for Godot*. Beckett's play was staged by the Welsh Drama Studio in 1969, a year after *The Protagonists* was performed; Alan McPherson played Estragon and Owen Garmon (who played J in BC's play) was Vladimir. I am grateful to Alan McPherson for these insights.

CASTRATE THE ENEMY . . . PYTHON ON ON ON (p. 51): See note to 'LE PYTHON LE PYTHON LE PY–', p. 98 above.

Besides, there are many . . . cries for mama (p. 51): Following this line in *Prot* 1 (p. 119) are the following lines (later struck through) in faulty Welsh; it is unclear whether the solecisms are intentional: 'Hiraeth, Duw cariad Duw. Mab y mynydd ond mae'n calon a'r y mynydd efor grug a'r adar man. Ydwyf innau oddi cartref yn gwneud cân'. 'Hiraeth' is a deep longing (often for home); 'Duw cariad Duw' is properly 'Duw cariad yw' – 'God is love' (from 1 John, 4:16). The remaining lines are from the final stanza of the famous lyric of exile and *hiraeth*, 'Nant y Mynydd', by John Ceiriog Hughes (1832–87).

I've been forgotten . . . something to say (p. 52): Annotation in *Prot* 6: 'Go → H – threaten him – whip'.

Since we're paid by the line . . . something to say (p. 52): On the evidence of *Prot* 6, excised in performance.

IT IS FORBIDDEN . . . NOT HAPPY AND CALM (p. 52): Possibly excised in performance: the evidence of *Prot* 6 is unclear.

There's a saying: 'Women and children, last' (p. 53): On the evidence of *Prot* 6, excised in performance.

It's getting late . . . round the roots (p. 54): Originally assigned to the Guard; reassigned to Z (more appropriately) in *Prot* 6.

I've strong teeth . . . eyes (p. 54): On the evidence of *Prot* 6, excised in performance.

Go on, go on, weep . . . In the Edict Maker's cell (pp. 54–5): On the evidence of *Prot* 6, excised in performance.

God, what a lovely place life is! (p. 54): On the evidence of *Prot* 6, excised in performance. Possibly an echo of Polly Garter's line in Dylan Thomas's *Under Milk Wood*: 'Oh, isn't life a terrible thing, thank God?'.

I know how I'd like to end it . . . his absence shakes me (pp. 55–6): On the evidence of *Prot* 6, excised in performance.

I can't do it . . . small boat (p. 56): On the evidence of *Prot* 6, excised in performance.

L, where are you? . . . grown-up son (pp. 56–7): On the evidence of *Prot* 6, these lines were transposed in performance to a position after L's 'Get to hell, away from me. You smell of the dungheap' (p. 54), and were followed by H's lines beginning 'Now I can take my time over studying' (p. 55).

myrrha, et gutta, et casia . . . **half-darkness (p. 57)**: On the evidence of *Prot* 6, excised in performance.

myrrha, et gutta, et casia a vestimentis tuis **(p. 57)**: Psalm 44:9–10 from the Clementine Latin Vulgate, included in the Roman Missal: 'Myrrha, et gutta, et casia a vestimentis tuis, a domibus eburneis: ex quibus delectaverunt te filiae regum in honore tuo'. In the Knox Version: 'Your garments are scented with myrrh, and aloes, and cassia; from ivory palaces there are harps sounding in your honour. Daughters of kings come out to meet you'. Once again, L begins her compassionate act of translating Z.

decore Indis florescere voluisti **(p. 57)**: From the prayer (in the 'Proper of Saints') in the Roman Missal giving thanks for the life of St Rose of Lima (1586–1617) – the first native of the Americas to be canonised by the Roman Catholic Church: 'Bonorum omnium largitor, omnipotens Deus, qui beatam Rosam, caelestis gratiae rore praeventam, virginitatis et patientiae decore Indis florescere voluisti: da nobis, famulis tuis; ut in odorem suavitatis eius currentes, Christi bonus odor effici mereamur'. L translates in the next line. The full translation runs: '[Almighty God, from whom cometh down every good and perfect gift, and who didst cause the dew of thy grace to fall early from heaven upon this blessed Rose,] making the same to blossom in the Indies, [as a flower whose loveliness was virginity and long-suffering, grant unto thy servants, who do run after the smell of her perfumes, worthily themselves to become a sweet savour unto Christ']. In her creative chronicle of her time on Bardsey Island, *Tide-race* (1962), BC includes three versions of her poem 'Rose of Lima' as an illustration of '[t]he making of a poem'; the third version runs: 'Rose of Lima! Rose of Lima! // The fragrance of your passing / Reminds me of the island / Which like a bride wears proudly / Perfumed with cassia myrrh and aloe / A jewel at the breast's hollow / Of pigeon-curving bone // This barbar-coloured, wave-worn pebble / Burnt with sea-light; clasp, exotic Rose // Warm rock for the palm, in your dark cell!' (p. 183).

I look everywhere . . . I look for signs! (p. 57): On the evidence of *Prot* 6, excised in performance. Cf. the entry for 6 May in BC's Ídhra journal for 1966, 'A Total Eclipse of the Sun' (NLW MS 21500E, p. 48): 'Cicada? No, now I think a cricket, from the bakery below. I look for signs; everywhere, I look for signs'.

Give me the gift . . . snows of India (p. 57): BC's adaptation of the entry, in French, for 20 June in her Ídhra journal for 1966, 'A Total Eclipse of the Sun' (NLW MS 21500E, p. 52):

'Donnez-moi les mots d'Afrique ou les singes de Sumatra ou les neiges d'Indie [*sic*] parce que je suis une femme vieille qui souffre de beaucoup de joi[e]' ('Give me the words of Africa or the monkeys of Sumatra or the snows of India, for I am an old woman who suffers from too much joy'). Rendering 'singes' ('monkeys') as 'sieges' is curious: it is possible that, on returning to her journal, BC misread (or saw a poetic fitness in misreading) 'singes' as 'sièges' ('seats'), and opted for the obsolete English cognate, 'sieges' – 'place[s] in which one has [one's] seat or residence; [seats] of rule, empires, etc' (*OED*).

In spring, she will be rutting-mad . . . almond blossom (p. 58): Cf. the entry under 7 February in BC's Ídhra journal for 1966, 'A Total Eclipse of the Sun' (NLW MS 21500E, p. 38), referring to one of the islanders: 'The maenad-Irini is rutting-mad these days – her breasts swell with the almond'. A 'maenad' is a 'Bacchante . . . a frenzied woman' (*OED*).

In February, the humming of bees . . . earthquake weather (p. 58): Cf. the entry under 7 February in BC's Ídhra journal for 1966, 'A Total Eclipse of the Sun' (NLW MS 21500E, p. 38): 'In the mountains northwards, there have been bad earthquakes: 3000 reported homeless. Areas that have been quaked never seem to regain their souls'; and the entry for 11 February: 'Unnaturally warm, strong gusts of wind during the night. Earthquake weather?'. The lines appeared posthumously in 'A Total Eclipse of the Sun', *Mabon* (Spring 1972), p. 11.

You say you have . . . by Jesus (p. 58): On the evidence of *Prot* 6, excised in performance.

Take your own advice (p. 58): On the evidence of *Prot* 6, excised in performance.

Like this double agent next to me (p. 59): On the evidence of *Prot* 6, altered in performance to 'Like this double agent up there'.

Like this double agent . . . swine with two faces (p. 59)
In *Prot* 1, opposite this line (p. 140), BC has written: 'Nikos
Kralis: (The Barbarians) ["]This clatter of the chains is the
only life there is["] (trans. David Posner)'. This is David Louis
Posner's translation of Manos (not Nikos) Kralis's poem,
'The Barbarians', which BC had recently encountered in *The
Voice of Cyprus: An Anthology of Cypriot Literature*, ed. Andónis
Decaválles et al. (New York: October House, 1966).

The last comfort gone . . . I hate (p. 60): On the evidence of
Prot 6, excised in performance.

la mission de sauver . . . la corruption **(p. 60)**: Translation:
'the mission to save the youth of today from immorality
and corruption. The educational and cultural objectives of
an anarchist crowd: to prepare enemies of the nation to
drive many young people into poverty, immorality and
corruption.' The evidence of *Prot* 5 and *Prot* 6 suggests
that the loudspeaker voice is Z's, though a Director should
have flexibility here.

Viole un cadavre avec la bénédiction! **(p. 60)**: 'Rape a corpse
with our blessing!'

They are the lucky ones (p. 60): Altered in *Prot* 6 to read:
'You're the lucky ones'.

A melancholic beach . . . All time is dangerous (p. 61): On
the evidence of *Prot* 6, excised in performance.

As women are (p. 61): On the evidence of *Prot* 6, excised in
performance.

It is the end of our time (p. 61): Cf. the opening of BC's Ídhra
journal for 1966, 'A Total Eclipse of the Sun' (NLW MS 21500E,
p. 28): 'It is the end of our time. These are the last months, weeks,
perhaps days, that we shall be free to sit in the sun. A terrible

change is about to take place. It has been foretold'. The lines appeared posthumously in 'A Total Eclipse of the Sun', *Mabon* (Spring 1972), p. 6, revised to read: 'A terrible change is about to take away our liberty. It has been foretold in the marketplace'. The first of the pair of letters Chamberlain passed to members of the cast and crew on the evening of the first performance of *The Protagonists* (see Introduction, pp. xlix–l above) concluded with the line 'It is the end of our time'.

imitate the sphinx cheaply (p. 61): On the evidence of *Prot* 6, 'cheaply' excised in performance.

I dream too much . . . anemones (p. 62): The lines appear in *PD*, p. 18 – 'I dream too much, over and over: I / wander far from home, and am unable / to find the way back / through farmland and empty barns: / lost, among alien people, in unbounded landscape // Against night-hauntings, an evocation: / narcissi, eucalyptus, fritillary / Poseidon! Hygaea!' – opposite 3 scored, striated rock forms. The image is dated 1968. Cf. the entry for 23 January in BC's Ídhra journal for 1966, 'A Total Eclipse of the Sun' (NLW MS 21500E, p. 34): 'Almond in bloom. Sheep cries are fecund, cats are mating. Same dream, repeated endlessly, of leaving home for ten minutes (fish on the stove, frying)[,] going too far, unable to find way back[,] always through barns, farmyards, fields . . . This is the spring, my depressed spirits sense it, lassitude, melancholy. The effort of these wild months is over, what now? Orpheus and Eurydice? I dream too much, anxiety nightmares, always lost, crowds of alien people, vast town or landscapes in which I wander, seeking. Roses, narcissi, eucalyptus, mandarin oranges, anemones the exact colour of my nightdress'. The passage appeared posthumously in 'A Total Eclipse of the Sun', *Mabon* (Spring 1972), p. 9.

paniyiri (p. 62): A Greek feast day, a festival.

Alms! Alms! . . . good for alms (p. 62): Cf. the entry for 20 June in BC's Ídhra journal for 1966, 'A Total Eclipse of the Sun' (NLW MS 21500E, p. 53): 'To the ancient of days, the ancient sybil, alms!'.

MAN . . . WAR (p. 63): A 'game' (as the Edict Maker has it) of verbal 'free association' that keys the play into psychoanalytical and Surrealist methods.

The sight of a flock of sheep . . . to silence (p. 64): An image rooted in the time BC spent on Esmé Firbank's farm on the slopes of the Glyderau, Snowdonia, North Wales in the early 1940s, recorded in her journal-essay, 'Mountains of Rock' (*The Welsh Review*, 4, 3 (September 1945), 190–7): 'The first sheep began to move down out of cloud, worming their way in small companies between the crags . . . Far bleating slowly changed to the full wailing of a flock in motion. From pockets of rock and steep gullies, in growing numbers, they streamed before the moving fanshape of men' (p. 191). The farm, Dyffryn, was made famous by Thomas Firbank's wartime bestseller, *I Bought a Mountain* (1940). BC incorporated the passage from 'Mountains of Rock' into *Tide-race* (1962), pp. 148–9, mapping mountain ground onto Bardsey Island.

No, not for a moment . . . reflexes (p. 64): On the evidence of *Prot* 6, excised in performance.

You are a person without will power (p. 64): Annotation in *Prot* 6: 'let him threaten J etc'.

I want a glass of water (p. 64): On the evidence of *Prot* 6, excised in performance.

So, you consider . . . brains? (p. 65): On the evidence of *Prot* 6, changed to '[Y]ou could use the gun on yourself' in performance.

I must have revenge . . . born (p. 65): On the evidence of *Prot* 6, excised in performance.

Are you planning . . . yourself? (p. 65): On the evidence of *Prot* 6, changed to 'Why not blow out your own brains[?]' in performance.

It happened to a man . . . steaming onto the grass (p. 65): Strongly suggestive (with the added prompt of H's word 'betrayed', two lines before) of the manner of Judas's death. According to Acts 1:18, his bowels 'gushed out' onto ground known thereafter as 'The Field of Blood' after he had fallen 'headlong' and 'burst asunder'.

Yes, compromise is the only solution (p. 65): On the evidence of *Prot* 6, excised in performance.

I'll take you to Italy (p. 66): On the evidence of *Prot* 6, excised in performance.

If the tablecloth . . . has to be now (p. 67): On the evidence of *Prot* 6, excised in performance.

It's the humane thing . . . for his own good (p. 68): On the evidence of *Prot* 6, excised in performance.

O: *Kyrie, eleison* (pp. 68-9): The two instances of '*Kyrie, eleison*' and of '*Christe, eleison*' given here to O are assigned to 'ALL' in *Prot* 6.

***Kyrie, eleison . . . Christe, eleison* (pp. 68-9)**: 'Lord, have mercy' and 'Christ, have mercy', which, as here, feature thrice in the Tridentine Mass of the Roman Rite.

***Gloria in excelsis Deo . . . bonae voluntatis* (p. 69)**: 'Glory to God in the highest and on earth peace, goodwill to all men/people': the second line of the hymn known as the 'Greater Doxology' and the 'Angelic Hymn', deriving from Luke 2:14.

In the Roman Rite, the hymn is part of the Mass and is sung, as here, after the Kyrie.

Loudspeaker, Z's voice **(p. 69)**: In neither *Prot* 5 nor *Prot* 6 is it clear precisely whose loudspeaker voice is meant at this point (the directions merely state 'Loudspeaker').

Loudspeaker, Z's voice . . . **a good bean soup (pp. 69–70)**: On the evidence of *Prot* 6, excised in performance.

Don't let it shock you! (p. 69): Cf. the first sentence of the Preface (p. 5).

As a deer for running water (p. 69): Psalm 41:2 (in the Knox Version): 'O God, my whole soul longs for you, as a deer for running water'.

Passports! . . .You took my papers, damn you! (p. 70): In 1965 on Ídhra, Chamberlain created a series of ten graphic works bearing the title 'The Black Bride'. As Maurice Cooke writes: 'On the last of the series, a collage, where the bride has become one with her white wedding dress and is being wrapped in pieces of cut newspaper in a version of late-cubist technique, [Chamberlain] writes simply "Voyage sans Passeport"'; 'The Painting of Brenda Chamberlain', *Anglo-Welsh Review*, 20, 46 (Spring, 1972), p. 12.

Posthumous laurels! . . . Immortality to – (p. 72): On the evidence of *Prot* 6, excised in performance.

VIVE LES RATS! (p. 72): 'Long live the rats!'

Are we to be left to die? (p. 72): On the evidence of *Prot* 6, excised in performance.

flow together into one stream **(p. 72)**: The final (double-sided) page of *Prot* 6 is torn in half at this point. On the reverse, the lines 'My forebears, Z' to the end are deleted. It is therefore impossible to say definitively what portion of the very end of the text survived in actual performance. Since O's lines here – 'My throat chokes on grey hair . . . grey hair' – recapitulate earlier lines, it seems reasonable to conclude that they were cut. O's capitalised edicts may have survived in performance.

DETERMINED TO SURVIVE, *repeated many times* (p. 73): Cf. *Prot* 4, p. 1 (verso): 'Possibly when house lights have come up and audience is leaving, "DETERMINED TO SURVIVE" could come over loud[s]peaker repeated in a number of languages until audience has left. Also, parts of edicts could be in various languages during course of play"'. BC has underlined 'could be in various languages' and has written: 'excellent! German French Italian Greek Welsh'.

There's your bone . . . death in all of us (p. 74): Identified as 'Last speech by Guard' by Alan McPherson in a photocopy of *Prot* 6 sent to me in 2011. This 'epilogue' is also identified as the Guard's in the earlier *Prot* 4 (p. 1b), in which the General makes an appearance: 'a figure strides down from rear seats of auditorium and onto bridge. Stops centre of bridge, facing actors. In costume and appearance he is unremarkable, but in the eyes of the other characters carries obvious authority. With snap of fingers he motions Guard to cut Z free, which Guard does, before resuming his former position. Another snap of the fingers, and [the Edict Maker] ushers J, H, A, O, and L and Z off stage right. "General" exits stage left past Guard, who comes to attention and salutes as he passes. Guard comes to centre stage, taking piece of paper from pocket. He proceeds to read the Epilogue from it. Then he crumples up the paper, places it carefully centre of bridge and exits stage right. Sound of practical door closing. House lights up'.

dry enough for your taste (p. 74): *Prot* 5 reads 'dry enough for your purpose', but the reading of the handwritten

'Conclusion' in *Prot* 6 is adopted here.

The dog buried it . . . dug up again (p. 74): Cf. the end of the first section ('The Burial of the Dead') of T. S. Eliot's *The Waste Land*: 'That corpse you planted last year in the garden, / Has it begun to sprout? Will it bloom this year? / Or has the sudden frost disturbed its bed? / Oh keep the Dog far hence, that's friend to men, / Or with his nails he'll dig it up again! / You! Hypocrite lecteur! – mon semblable – mon frère!'.

Light a candle . . . death in all of us (p. 74): Cf. the entry for 7 March in BC's Ídhra journal for 1966, 'A Total Eclipse of the Sun' (NLW MS 21500E, p. 46): 'I fill the house with flowers, open the windows, buy tall honey candles. I light one in the living room window, not only for the death of Him but for the death in all of us. An emperor moth beats at the window softly, like a timid child. I let it into the house, and draw it'. Annotation in *Prot* 6 at the end of the 'Conclusion': 'music / parade + exit'.

Appendix 1

'Theatre Plan to Boost Welsh Drama'

North Wales Chronicle, 26 September 1958, p. 7 (not attributed, but the journalist is probably Alan Twelves).

The actor-producer who is leading the Welsh Drama Studio, a theatre workshop plan, in Bangor told us this week that one of the aims was to promote Welsh drama into the European scene. This could be the beginning of a Welsh National Theatre in North Wales.

I spoke to Mr David Lyn, formerly with the Royal Shakespeare Company and a member of the Welsh Theatre Company, who has made many television appearances, in his home, Tŷ Hir, in Upper Llanfairpwll.

He explained why he had toned his hair to a rich Teutonic gold. 'It's for a Welsh-language serial, *Lleifior*, an adaptation of Islwyn Ffowc Elis's book, *Cysgod y Cryman* [The Shadow of the Sickle] which the BBC is filming for television, and in which I play a German ex-prisoner of war who returns to Wales after the war to take part in the agricultural revolution,' he said.

The Welsh Drama Studio, he said, envisaged production opportunities for original plays by Welsh authors. 'The scene should become as constructive and comprehensive and totally Welsh as the actors are, not a theatre with Welsh accents. It must be so if it is going to be a natural expression of the culture of the people.'

Gwyn Thomas, Emyr Humphreys, Alun Llywelyn-Williams and John Gwilym Jones are taking an interest in what the Welsh Drama Studio is doing.

The Arts Council will become involved and there are plans to buy a former chapel in Caellepa, Bangor. 'The chapel would be ideal, being theatrical in its conception, and a splendid base for the workshop activities,' said Mr Lyn.

Development

He came to North Wales to take part in the development of the Welsh theatre. He had been attached to the Welsh Theatre Company on and off for four or five years and later came to the conclusion that there was no committed policy that was coherent and cohesive.

What he wants to achieve through a workshop plan is somewhere where Welsh authors can have a chance to try out their ideas. Such things have already been happening in England. Mr Lyn decided on the Bangor base as having a nucleus of a cultural community.

'Welsh authors seem terribly timid, and I think we must attempt to draw them forward,' he said.

Positive

I asked why an actor who was making a good living in England should quit the big centres and come to North Wales. 'It was this feeling that there could be a renaissance; that something significant could be caused to happen, I suppose,' replied Mr Lyn. He began to think that he was contributing little as an actor to what was happening. So the Welsh Theatre Company called him; then came the drama studio idea.

He also became a BBC contract artist, but still had time on his hands . . . This was how the Welsh Drama Studio suggested itself.

The first essay of the group will be on October 11 and 12 at the Prichard-Jones Hall, Bangor: Brenda Chamberlain's first play, *The Protagonists*. It was inspired by Miss C.'s being caught up in the Greek military coup, but it goes deeper than the Greek situation, broadening into the universality of the nature of power, tyranny and corruption. For the play, David Lyn, who is producing, has drawn together an exciting group of young professional actors.

Could the forces of a Welsh National Theatre be actors like Donald Houston, Glyn Houston and Richard Burton? 'No; as I see it these fine actors – with due respect – now belong to the English tradition; our object is to initiate things here in Wales,' said Mr Lyn. But, he added, the movement would not be too proud to 'accept their glamour, their prestige from time to time'.

The Welsh Drama Studio has plans for a Welsh-language pantomime based on an Arthurian story and for a Christmas play for Children, Robert Bolt's *The Thwarting of Baron Bolligrew*.

As well as financial security, it is necessary for the actor to have artistic security. And in his thinking on actors Mr Lyn does not dismiss the amateur. 'There is a wealth of experience among the amateurs, but a problem will be to make the prospect of crossing over sufficiently attractive to drag the best ones away from being civil servants or butchers,' he said.

Eisteddfod

Mr Lyn believes the National Eisteddfod offers little hope of anything bold or new happening in drama. 'This is the seat of the "Cymry fach [*sic*]," he declared. 'There are the people who hold fast to the old traditions with great nostalgia, and talk folksy things. The Eisteddfod is a great place socially, but nothing much happens on the platform.' He likened the eisteddfod scene to 'a sort of Christmas carolling'.

But the new upsurge, which Mr Lyn senses, must spring from Wales itself; it cannot be imported. 'There must be no English acting with Welsh accents,' he insists. It would be all right to use the glamour of established 'fugitive' Welsh actors, but the national movement must not rely or base its aspirations on them.

Appendix 2

The Protagonists – Formal Rehearsal Schedule*

August 1968	Sun.	25th	Prichard Jones Hall, University College of North Wales, Bangor	Technical Conference	2pm
	Wed.	28th	"	Recording, etc	7.30–10.30pm
Sept.	Sun.	1st	P-J. Hall	Rehearsal	2–10.30pm
	Tues.	3rd	"	"	7.30–10.30pm
	Wed.	4th	"	"	7.30–10.30pm
	Thurs.	5th	"	"	7.30–10.30pm
	Sun.	8th	"	"	2–10.30pm
	Tues.	10th	"	"	7.30–10.30pm
	Wed.	11th	"	"	7.30–10.30pm
	Thurs.	12th	"	"	7.30–10.30pm
	Sun.	15th	"	"	2–10.30pm
	Tues.	17th	"	"	7.30–10.30pm
	Thurs.	19th	"	"	7.30–10.30pm
	Sun.	22nd	"	"	2–10.30pm
	Tues.	24th	"	"	7.30–10.30pm
	Thurs.	26th	"	"	7.30–10.30pm
	Mon.	30th	"	"	7.30–10.30pm
October	Wed.	2nd	Old Student Common Room	Rehearsal	7.30–10.30pm
	Sun	6th	P-J. Hall	"	2–10.30pm
	Mon.	7th	"	"	7.30–10.30pm
	Tues.	8th	"	"	7.30–10.30pm
	Thurs.	10th	"	Dress Rehearsal	2pm–
	Fri.	11th	"	Dress Rehearsal and Performance	2pm–
	Sat.	12th	"	Performance	2pm–

* From Alan McPherson's acting script; National Library of Wales, ex 2735.

Appendix 3

'Well, I'll just say there were lovely flowers there':
Brenda Chamberlain interviewed by Alan McPherson

Forecast (University College of North Wales, Bangor
student newspaper), May 1968, pp. 18–19

Brenda Chamberlain was born in Bangor. After leaving
school she spent six months in Copenhagen where she first
saw modern paintings. She spent five years as a painting
scholar at the Royal Academy Schools in London. After her
marriage she assisted in the work of the Caseg Press, run by
her husband, which specialised in the printing of broadsheets
in collaboration with the poet Alun Lewis.

Her poetry began to appear in many periodicals,
including *The Dublin Magazine*, *The Welsh Review*, *Botteghe
Oscure* (Italy), *Poetry Chicago*, *New Directions* (New York),
The New Yorker, and *The New York Times*. As an unpublished
collection, *The Green Heart* won the Arts Council (Welsh
Committee) Poetry Award in 1956.

Before moving finally to Greece she lived for fifteen years
on the island of Bardsey, writing and painting.

She has held many exhibitions in both England and
Wales. Her play, *The Protagonists*, will be produced by
David Lyn in October and will be performed in the round
in P[richard]-J[ones]. Hall. The Arts Council are backing the
play, and it seems very possible that after its premiere in
Bangor the play will be produced in London by one of the
leading theatrical companies.

Alan McPherson interviews her here:

How did you come to be in Greece in the first place?
I went by chance; it was an unplanned journey. Someone said, 'I've got a car and a seat; we're going to drive right through Europe to the sun; would you like to come? Destination Athens.'

Was it on this visit to Greece that you went to Hydra?
No, I only got as far as Athens because promptly the car ran into the back of a Greek lawyer whose car was stationary at the lights. I just came home because I was badly smashed; but I returned as soon as I could.

To Hydra?
Yes. I was going to write a book about a specific subject which I had been brooding about for a long time and for some reason I decided it had to be written on a Greek island. And it was by chance that I was offered a house on this island, and when I got there I found it was exactly what I needed and so I stayed there from April to November, until the book was finished.

Was that A Rope of Vines*?*
Yes. Then I brought it to London and came straight to the publisher. I had to see to all the drawings and then I went back and was there six years.

You were there during the coup?
Yes. I'd returned to Wales in the winter before, and I got back to Greece last year the beginning of the week of the coup, which was on the Friday. I got there about Monday, you see, so I was there literally three or four days before the coup.

What was it like?
I was just in Athens waiting to go to the island, waiting for the next ship, and it was absolutely quiet and normal. There was no sign of any unrest or disturbance. It was just this uncanny total negativeness. I got up in the morning after the coup, didn't know there'd been a coup; a woman in the house above

came and leaned over the wall and spoke to me and didn't mention a word. The children weren't at school, but I thought it must be a holiday, you know. I just didn't realise what was wrong. The children had all been sent back from school and they were all around the place; that was the uncanny silence. Nobody's transistors were on; it was very strange, but I didn't know until I went down actually to the port. I was told; and then I saw of course that the men were sitting at the café tables in absolute silence, just sitting, and one or two transistors going. And everybody just listening to the hourly bulletins – it was totally negative. You see, everything was, 'If you do this, SHOT ON SIGHT.' 'If you do that you'll be SHOT ON SIGHT.' And it was everything, so that nothing could happen, you see.

And what sort of things would you have been shot on sight for doing?
Well, there was a curfew for one thing – six o'clock I think it was in the evening; anyone out after that would be shot. It was so lunatic, you see; it was everything, there was no movement because nobody could leave the country; they couldn't move about within Greece. They couldn't go to a relation's house without telling the police; they used to tell the police if they moved at all. You see, there must be no movement. Then of course all the guns had to be handed in; all the guns were called in, because every man owned a gun. No man had a gun or weapon.

Did the police give you any trouble?
No, but there was this feeling as you walked through the port – shopping, for instance. It was like being reassessed, because people I didn't know – townspeople – were all just sitting around; and I know I was being reassessed, as a foreigner, and I did actually hear one man say to another, 'She's all right.' You see, I heard that; I mean they were just chatting; it was a weird feeling, it was like going through an examination of some sort. It was obvious that as a foreigner

you should just stay quietly at home; naturally they were terribly disturbed, and as a foreigner you were nothing to do with it. It seemed rather necessary to keep as quiet as possible and definitely not to talk publicly. I mean, there was one man in particular who is an informer – he simply became more dangerous, but he was dangerous before as well.

Had you had any idea you were going to write a play before you went back that time?
I'd never, never wanted to write a play.

You'd never written a play before?
I never wanted to; I never thought of using that form, never. I thought of film, funnily enough, not about this at all; but I'd thought of a film I wanted to make in Greece – but never a play.

When you started writing, did you know it was going to be a play?
Not at all. First I wrote things like the beginning of a play – you know, I wrote bits down. And when I went to Léros for the second time, I wrote a few more bits. Léros is the detention island.

Where the political prisoners are?
Yes. And for instance, that part at the beginning when someone says, 'the mountains whose geography we shall never be allowed to know' – well, this came from various views of the marvellous mountains, actually on the next island, but it looked as though it was part of the same island. To me it was like a prison, the whole island – I began to feel like a prisoner, too.

When did you realise it was a play?
There was this friend, an American, who was writing a play himself. I read a bit of his play, and he read these fragments and said, 'My God! How strong; this is a play!' and he spoke with great conviction, you see. I just went home; it was as though a key had been turned on something. I just saw the whole thing

come – it just began, and every day it never stopped after that. At eight o'clock every morning I just sat and put it down – it came so fast that I always had one of those little books, these little Greek notebook things, and when I went down into the port or anywhere, I had one of these with me, and it was just coming the whole time. People were speaking – it was direct speech. I never wrote any happenings, any direct description; it just happened through their voices. It was terribly exciting.

It was so strange to me because it was a form I knew nothing of, and I kept thinking there must be a catch in this, there must be something wrong here. I was checking back all the time, seeing if they were speaking out of character, but they were always themselves, you know; I thought it can't be true that this person is saying this, but it always keyed in in a strange way.

The play is deeply concerned with the evils of fascism. Do you see it as propaganda?
It's no propaganda; it was simply the result of enormous pressure and misery, and being absolutely unable to do a thing. I couldn't paint, I couldn't draw, I could do nothing for months – you know, this happens – and so I knew that something must be on the way.

I couldn't believe this was the end. Nothing would come. The atmosphere was so sterile because the year before everybody had been working in the foreign colony, very hard, and they'd all dispersed. It was something that was in the air, long before the coup. Two Greek friends the year before had told me something awful was going to happen and I didn't believe them – but they told me certainly something was coming and they both got out, you see.

Did you make it public in Greece that you'd written the play?
No, I kept it completely secret. I was very careful about the fact that I went to Léros. A Greek friend advised me when I came back. He said, 'Don't talk about having been there' – quite

apart from having written anything. He said, 'Don't talk.' So as a joke I said, 'Well, I'll just say there were lovely flowers there.' And he said, 'Yes, you just say that.' And so I said, 'Very beautiful and very pretty; lovely flowers there.' My family – the Greek peasants I was living with – knew I was writing a play, but they were peasant people and never spoke about it.

They used to look over my shoulder – they saw the drawings and the caged figures – but the dialogue meant nothing to them. I didn't want to implicate them, so I never spoke in case of any danger to them, and I always hid it every time I went out in the bottom of my trunk. Before I came out I read it to six friends I trusted absolutely and knew wouldn't gossip, and then I sent two copies out through Cyprus and brought one openly in my bag – because they did go through my suitcase at the last moment. They called me back and opened it – it was a good thing the play was in my shoulder bag.

Tell me more about the feeling behind the play.
The play was the result of total inhibition, of being made to feel so inhibited as a foreigner – as somebody who was living there and who wanted to go on living there in spite of everything. You had the feeling all the time that you could be caught and put out for literally anything. For instance, if you rested your leg on a chair – you know they have these very hard seats in Greece – you would be hauled up by the police for that. If your dress was slightly transparent and could be seen through, that was another thing. One really thought about all these things: is my skirt transparent? – it was madness.

You go out here and you don't think if there are policemen following you and watching you – you have no idea.

The poor men, the peasants! They're an incredibly exuberant people, and very noisy, and if they shouted or laughed or sang they were told to shut up. You know every

Greek breaks glasses – the breaking of glasses is phenomenal – but suddenly this was a barbarous thing and must not be done. This breaking glasses was either an insult or a congratulation, you see; it's a tricky business – you can be mortally offended or congratulated: if you've done a marvellous dance they break a glass at your feet, or if they want to insult you they break a glass – and that was suddenly not allowed.

This is why for me the play has this violence, because it was a breaking out – I had to break out in some way. One night everybody thought I was completely crazy. The play was finished; I don't know why but I had it on me one night in the port and I was with old friends who had come from Cyprus, and I very seldom go to a Taverna. We went to a Taverna and I suppose I'd had too much retsina; I started reading from it at the top of my voice. This was crazy but there was this feeling – you had to break out.

On Sundays they have this thing with loudspeakers in the squares, just battering at the people; one just hears this voice – its indoctrination. At the end of the play the edicts are distorted to make them sound comic, but they are taken from the newspapers: that thing about the python and 'castrate the enemy' – that was actually in the Athens news. Sounds mad.

What do you think is going to happen in Greece – from what you know of the people?
I've no idea – you see the civil war must have been so terrible and it's within memory. You never hear anyone speak of it, it was dreadful – actually fighting their brothers – and I think they probably feel that anything is better than that again. That must be part of it. Anything is better than the slaughter of the children – all those children that were taken away to Yugoslavia and never came back.

When the King went it was heartbreakingly pathetic. That day in my family the wife said, 'Why, why, why has he gone?' It was as though a father or an uncle, someone they respected enormously, had just deserted them. It was just after the trouble in Cyprus and he'd gone. And Rome was so impossibly far away and in somewhere, they thought, called Italy. It was inconceivable.

And this same woman when the Cyprus troubles were on: I just happened to say Cyprus was an island; she said, 'It's not.' I said, 'But it is'; she said, 'It's not.' I couldn't find an atlas anywhere and she went out and asked her husband who was painting the house, and said, 'Brenda says Cyprus is an island.' And because he was a man, she took his word for it.

On this island in particular all the menfolk go to the ends of the earth – they always have done and because of that the rest of the world doesn't exist for them. You'd think it would exist more, but it doesn't; it's just the island.

They don't speak about Athens, just the port of Piraeus because they've all got masses of family in Piraeus. All that exists is the island and Piraeus. The clampdown was easier because of this, because if you're scattered over an infinite number of islands with quite a distance in between – 14, 16, 18 hours by ship between some; no ships, no mail, no radio except their own – it's very efficient and so simple. When the newspapers did come they censored them – any relevant thing they cut out, they cut out the page.

Now about the play.
I did it for Greece – I wrote it for Greece – as something to do positively for Greece. I didn't know positively at first what form it would take, but as soon as it began to come out like this I realised it was a play, which isn't political propaganda in any sense, but, I suppose, an emotional reaction to the situation. I felt I had to do something since there was no taking to the hills. You know, we would have gone to the hills definitely had the King been able to get a message through – we would

122

have just taken to the mountains in northern Greece. I didn't work it out; it was an emotional reaction to the beastliness of the situation – I just hope that it will come across in the play.

There isn't any direct political message in the play, is there?
No, no, because I know nothing of politics and I suppose I'm not interested. I'm just interested in how people react, in what people do and feel and think.

The funny thing was that when I read it to my six friends on Hydra, two of them – one a Frenchman and the other a Greek, close friends – they were absolutely outraged and nearly flew at me when I had finished reading and were absolutely so angry. They shouted, 'You've gone too far, all this politics; you must take out all these edicts.' It was very extraordinary – they were so aggressive they shook me. But both of them, when I rationalised about it, had visa trouble. They said, 'All this talk of visas, all these edicts: absolute nonsense – it's not true.' They were the two of the six who really had problems – one with the police to stay in, and the other to get a visa to get out. They were petrified. The play can't come across here in the same way. The minute I said the first sentence they were absolutely shaken and said, 'For God's sake lower your voice,' because I was reading in a garden – a large garden, in a language none of the neighbours understood, but the whole thing was so loaded for them.

Now we must try and get this across by artificial means – by artifice.

By bombarding the audience with edicts?
No. I don't know about bombarding them – it has to be subtle, an insidious thing. You've got to creep into their minds before you start bombarding, but they have got to be convinced in some way of the reality of it, that it isn't just a play but something that could affect them.

What about presentation? Do you want to use a traditional stage?
No, no. The action of the play must be as close to the audience as possible – it should be in and around and among them. The audience should be around the cages so that they can begin to imagine that they are in the same situation. That they perhaps are in a cage or about to be put in a cage – or they are even part of the cell block. It's cutting out the sense of background so that the mind should be able to imagine the setting – the island and the prison – and not thinking of a backcloth and wings. It must be Léros or any arid island.

Appendix 4

Lindsay Hutchinson and Simon Sherwin,
Review of *The Protagonists* in Performance

Forecast (University College of North Wales, Bangor
student newspaper), October 1968, p. 12.

The Protagonists is certainly a very enjoyable piece of
entertainment. Indeed, what play using the forms of
classical Greek drama, vaudeville and circus in the manner
of Saunders, Beckett, Ionesco, Weiss and Sartre could fail to
engage its audience, particularly when presented with the
colour and energy of David Lyn's production? But despite
this, despite the plethora of images that the script sparks
off, there is no fuel, nothing catches fire and we get the
unpleasant feeling that we've been had by art for art's sake.

The play is set in a Greek prison and the characters are
six political detainees, their guard and the 'Edict Maker'.
What action there is involves an experiment in which the
prisoners wrestle for the power of a gun which turns out to
be an impotent force among these insane wrecks of humanity.
The prisoners are represented as wild animals performing to
the crack of the guard's whip; they are also represented as
subversive, destructive, anarchic rodents. One would expect
some dialectical interchange between these antagonistic
symbols. But there is none – they are given vicariously at their
face value. Similarly, we are presented with the possibility that
the nameless person played by Jeff Thompson is or is not a
priest and that the woman played by Sophia Michopoulou is
or is not his mother. We are given reasons to believe both that
she symbolises Greece and that she doesn't symbolise Greece.
We are drenched with water symbols which can be construed

as either the Greek islands, the sea around them, or the forces that fertilise them. On top of all these, and many more, confusions of the text, we are subjected to every alienation technique in the book. And to what purpose? Alienation is a device by which we are made to stand back from, and see in a new light, things that are being taken for granted. Yet the author deliberately refrains from giving us anything to stand back from, and we have to conclude that they are being used merely for the immediate entertainment effect.

What made the performance of this play so indubitably enjoyable must be put down to the brilliant aplomb with which the cast raced over this crumbling intellectual terrain. I have rarely seen so ingenious and attractive a set so cleverly used. Problems of actor interpretation arose due to ambiguities in the text as to whether they were playing individual people or poetic archetypes. Phredd McPherson's delightfully roguish guard was fairly literally played, whereas Ian Lean's Machiavellian Edict Maker succeeded as a well-sustained melodramatic caricature of a dictatorship. Interpretation was harder for the group of prisoners. Gwyn Parry, Owen Garmon and Gray Evans were, more or less, interchangeable elements of a chorus, while Jeff Thompson, Sophia Michopoulou and Vassili were coextensive with this abstract group and had also to maintain personal identities. Notwithstanding, taking each crevasse as they came to it, they managed to capture the audience with the strength and consistency of some very persuasive acting.

The Protagonists is Brenda Chamberlain's first play and rich as it undoubtedly is in poetic and dramatic inventiveness it is self-indulgent, has no coherence and makes no sense as a whole. The play is ostensibly about Greece and its suppressive military dictatorship, and the programme encourages us to believe that it is an expression of solidarity with the people of Greece. But the play refuses to see the facts in political terms.

The protagonists are the dictator on one hand and on the other a bunch of ideologically bankrupt liberal intellectuals who are motivated only by nostalgia. Miss Chamberlain says in the programme, 'it is no propaganda; it was simply the result of enormous pressure and misery, and being absolutely unable to do a thing.' But what solidarity can Miss Chamberlain claim with the Greek people when she exempts herself even from helping their propaganda? *The Protagonists* seems to stand in the same relation to Greece, to quote Marx, 'as onanism to sexual love.' Moreover (with respect to the dictatorship) to quote Mao, 'everything reactionary is the same; if you don't hit it, it won't fall.'

The North Wales Association for the Arts, with which I had a fleeting role, exists to preserve the coterie nature of modern self-expression. Music for discriminating people is really what it does best, but since there is a committee for drama, drama there occasionally must be.

The Protagonists was apparently about the effect that totalitarian extremism had, both on the oppressor and [on] the oppressed. Miss Chamberlain seemed to be suggesting that each contained within himself the other, and that all we can do is preserve our right to lonely lyricism. The guard, I think, was absurd that we may reflect how absurd such people do seem, and the prisoners numbered that we may realise how we lose our identity when such things go on. The play was full of allegory, comic relief and all sorts of things that discriminating people love to discriminate about.

The play was also incoherent, and here I think we may discover the real relationship between the North Wales Association for the Arts, the author in exile from Hydra and the fascist coup in Greece. Modern politics, in Peking, in Mexico, in Grosvenor Square or in Greece are, for the bourgeois audience, incoherent. Their newspapers present the antic behaviour of civil guards, red guards, long-haired hooligans, colonels and labour MPs; their drama presents Phredd comic, John Owen Hughes [Owen Garmon] serious and Jeff Thompson neurotic.

The sustained hysteria of the play may be fairly seen as a reflection of what a person who likes living in Greece makes of the spectacle of three quarters of the world's population throwing off the yoke of the other quarter.

Rehashing the clichés of sado-masochistic behaviour and cribbing from Dostoyevski and Koestler, the play was an awful indulgence for a predominantly middle-aged, middle-class audience. The applause was of that nervous kind which follows contact with Debussy's lyricism, or more pertinently, Beethoven's madness. I was left thinking of Joy Roberts going for the scaffolding to Maintenance and for the straight-jacket to the madhouse.

Damian Walford Davies is Rendel Professor of English and Head of the Department of English and Creative Writing at Aberystwyth University. He is the author, most recently, of *Cartographies of Culture: New Geographies of Welsh Writing in English* (University of Wales Press, 2012) which offers new interpretations of Chamberlain's life and work. He wrote the introduction to the 2012 Library of Wales edition of Chamberlain's 1964 novel, *The Water-Castle*, also published by Parthian.

The Water-castle
BRENDA CHAMBERLAIN

Love and discord in post-war Germany, as a Welsh woman travels with her French husband to meet her former lover, a German count.

ISBN 9781908069795/ £8.99

A Rope of Vines – Journal from a Greek Island is a beautiful, personal account of the time spent by Brenda Chamberlain on the Greek Island of Ydra in the early 1960s.

ISBN 9781905762866/ £7.99

A Rope of Vines
Journal from a Greek Island
BRENDA CHAMBERLAIN
LIBRARY OF WALES

BRENDA CHAMBERLAIN
ARTIST&WRITER

JILL PIERCY

The first full-length biography, drawing upon extensive research gathered from public and private collections and from interviews with Chamberlain's friends in Britain, Germany and Greece.

ISBN 9781906998233/ £20.00

PARTHIAN

Lightning Source UK Ltd.
Milton Keynes UK
UKOW030615020513

210068UK00003B/8/P